life
mastery
decoded

IOANNIS TZIVANAKIS

ITV

CONTENT

For Her Teaching

"Men first feel necessity, then look for utility, next attend to comfort, still later amuse themselves with pleasure, thence grow dissolute in luxury, and finally go mad and waste their substance."

Giambattista Vico

Introduction

The decoding of life mastery is not necessarily easy, but at the same time it is clear and transparent, and given *by life itself*.

Therefore, it is necessary to let life in its wholeness into our healthy body and mind through open and perceptive receptivity.

After an introduction to the subject of the book in the prologue, in the first part of the book we find the basics of the intelligence of change, on which all life and the entire manifested reality are based in their becoming and happening.

The two important keys for intelligent and personally meaningful life control can be found in the second part of the book.

In the third and most comprehensive part we dive into the essence and significance of the six master acts of life, which also include the twenty most important life skills.

Penetration into the essence of the good life, the significance of the life forces for intelligent action and the supreme determining power of emotions are the main contents of the fourth and last part, in which all the life mastery keys also come together:

For a multilayered adulthood and the deeper or higher dimensions of life.

Then, in the epilogue, we conclude by presenting the twofold meaning of life as it is given by *reality*.

Prologue

The Fulfilling Life

Even though life mastery certainly does not mean anything small, since it refers to life as a whole and should certainly include substantial knowledge and skills, it can be understood more narrowly or more broadly.

Life mastery can be simple(r) if life conditions are simple and not overloaded with excessive goals and a psychologically destructive greed for more and more. At the same time, a rightly praised common sense and an unclouded self-understanding and knowledge of oneself are important prerequisites for this.

Life mastery can be simple(r) also when not much is needed for basic life satisfaction, because the everyday small and ordinary can be recognized, felt and enjoyed as a miraculous event just as much as a masterful musical composition, an aesthetically moving painting or a world-changing scientific breakthrough.

Unfortunately, however, the important fundamental and essential knowledge and abilities for life are not always (sufficiently) taught and transmitted in our culture of education, upbringing and living.

And even if it is communicated and encouraged or required from the outset, general life conditions and personal and biographically conditioned paths of growth and destiny often do not allow important life skills to be adequately and sufficiently experienced and internalized, whereby at least a rudimentary mastery of life can be achieved.

Finally, many who are basically doing well in life wish for *clarity*, *knowledge* and *realizable growth opportunities* to complete their life satisfaction because some important issues and dimensions are *still missing*, or to deepen it continuously because the inner urge to live and be is *not* yet truly *satisfied*.

Many play out a thought experiment, half for fun and half for real interest, to figure out or work out what can be used to identify what a good life is.

What does this thought experiment consist of? It consists in imagining in what words, when we already feel we have arrived at the end of life, we would summarize the life we have lived.

Through such an idea, if we really feel it and take it seriously, we may indeed be confronted with the challenge of finding out and knowing (1) what is a *good* life or even *the* good life, and (2) how to *realize* it.

By *decoding* life mastery, we find out,

(a) *what* life mastery consists of,

(b) what *master acts of life* and what *life skills* are required for it, and

(c) by what *milestones* and by what *states of life* it becomes apparent what degree and quality of life mastery is *realized*.

Part I:
The Great Mother
Of Becoming

1. The River Of Reality

If we look at our world and perhaps examine it more closely or observe it a little more curiously, we can see that among a gigantic multitude of properties which characterize our world... and even constitute it, i.e. determine it in its essence, one property is everywhere and continuously present and active....

In this gigantic panorama, which for us humans is composed of matter and consciousness or of the physical, the psychic or mental and the spiritual, in this interplay of the conceivable with the miraculous and of the banal with the extraordinary, one basic event stands out; ...one main act permeates all being. Well; ... at least almost all being!

What is this basic event? The answer cannot surprise. It is namely *change*. I mean the fact that our world - including ourselves - is in constant change; in the process of the incessant and also unstoppable becoming and passing away.

This is certainly not a new insight; not even a special, let alone subtle observation! In order to detect constant change, it is quite sufficient if we take an immediate and short look into the magnificent spectacle of nature, into the everyday amoeba-like transformations of our civilized human society or perhaps also into our all too familiar and multifaceted inner life.

Whether it is the seasons dancing rather confused steps and rhythms in the last decades, whether it is the economic turbulences in a now confusingly hectic world or the unfathomably complex causes of our emotional mutability, change hides and takes place in all dimensions and in all manifestations of our existence.

2. Emergence, Becoming, Decay

"Everything is in flux", Heraclitus said two and a half thousand years ago. Everything changes. And constantly.

Again and again, the question arises in me as to why everything is constantly changing. And the best answer that then comes to me is that change must be an immanent basic feature of nature, an inviolable physical primordial law.

In the results or rather observations of physical research, which seems to have reached its limits long ago, change can be detected even in the smallest building blocks of all matter. Whether these are the electrons or quarks or superstrings or still other smaller, still unnamed and perhaps also still more unfathomable particles or other entities or realities... In a spatially gigantic vastness of unfathomable extent the building blocks of which everything consists are in motion. They move, so it seems, according to – even if finally not easily determinable – natural laws. This movement, this absence of lifeless stillness and stagnation triggers and produces change.

So, the physical fact of movement could be understood as a kind of answer to the first why of constant change. Only, ...a further answer, namely to the following why, which would be "Why and by what this movement exists or originates?", is not in sight. Certainly, one could continue the whole matter and claim or assume that the necessity of movement of the smallest matter particles results from the existence of an enormous energy quantity, wherever it comes from! Others again would find the reverse order more valid: Energy originates only by movement. Hm...

However. The why or the whys remain untouched in their questioning essence, gallop on unperturbed and forcefully and lead inevitably to the question which already Leibniz put in the following formulation and which is able to burst a stubborn and megalomaniac mind, namely: Why is there something at all and not rather nothing?

However, we do not want to be impressed by it now, since these first or last philosophical questions do not represent the object of our treatment. Instead we accept the factual fact that everything changes constantly, since we apparently cannot change this! We come to terms with it, embrace it as a fact, possibly even affirmatively and joyfully, and take part - calmly would be my suggestion - in this spectacular and breathtaking change machinery, everyone maximizing the personal happiness and realizing the personal values in her and his own way.

We have no choice, i.e. we cannot deny nor repress or ignore the fact that we participate in incessant change with body and soul or are completely a part of change ourselves! Even if we have not decided it. Or maybe this question does not arise at all?

As human beings we are a splendidly diverse example of multidimensional change; because we are living organisms and as such we exemplify a more intensive and therefore more obvious version of manifesting change than inorganic, i.e. lifeless, "life"-incapable matter would be able to do!

The physical forces which work in the inorganic as well as in the organic matter and trigger and also control the process of change are the same.

Beyond that there are of course also the spheres of the spiritual and the psychic or mental life and further still those of imagination and dreaming or possible psychic and metaphysical realms, in which the forces or laws creating change seem to differ from those of our physical universe.

But in all these spheres where becoming, passing away, and coming into being occur, the process of change remains identical. No matter where or how change occurs, the act that takes place is essentially the same. This becomes very clear to us when we get a clear picture of what change actually is.

What exactly takes place or happens that we call change?

3. The Inner Logic Of Change

Change is the process or happening within which something becomes something else. For example, a bare winter tree that transforms into a rich green, summer tree splendor, a crawling caterpillar that transforms into a flying butterfly, a tired human body that vibrates with fresh energy through sleep and movement, a luminous speck of dust that changes its spatial coordinates flying in the air, a sheep newly born on wobbly feet that after some time treads uneven ground with captivating certainty, a romantic lake that after a long drought degenerates into a huge dry hole, or a shy silent girl who after thirty years mutates into a powerful manager - just to name a few examples.

The definition of 'change' as the happening within which something becomes something else means that everything, some or at least a part of the totality that constitutes a something not yet changed becomes something else, a "new" something.

"...we had no say about coming into existence: we just woke up and found ourselves in a world."

Bryan Magee

'Becoming-something-else-or-other' includes various possibilities, which can be both qualitative and quantitative.

4. How Does Anything Change?

If I increase with regard to my body mass, the kind of change is quite obvious. This kind of change, where primarily – at a given time – something is added energetically and permanently to an x, comprises the category or family of the *additive changes*.

In the opposite case, if something is primarily – at a given time – energetically and permanently removed from an x, then we would speak of the family of *subtractive changes*. This would be the case, for example, if I remove all the dust from my study with a wet and absorbent wipe.

Finally, the *transformative changes* form the third and last family. In this type of change, the focus is primarily on the order transformation of the energetic accumulation that makes up a something in its entirety. In the last mentioned example my freshly dusted study causes a pleasant change in my state of mind. So in this case *primarily* my state of mind is transformed at a given time. For example, if I felt foggy before, after cleaning up my state of mind was refreshed at the same time.

A transformative change is primarily about the fact that all in all nothing is removed or taken away from a something or from an entity and also that nothing is added to it, but that this entity transforms itself, i.e. the structure or configuration of all partial entities, which exactly make it up as a whole, changes. This then is essentially a case of *restructuring*.

5. The Spectrum Of Change

In each of these above-mentioned types of change, something changes exclusively additively, subtractively or transformatively *only primarily*.

So, if I clean up the study, as in the last example, because I want to feel better as a result, we can speak of a primarily *transformative* change, namely that of my *state*, because that is the change I was concerned with in the first place or at least directly.

The other change, that of the cleanliness of the study, we can call indirect or instrumental.

Even beyond that, there may be additional changes that occur in parallel with and caused by a directly intended or instrumentally used change.

So let's say I share my study with someone else, and in my zeal for cleanliness, I remove a crumpled sheet suitable for the wastebasket and lying on the floor in the unmistakable knowledge that I am doing something good.

The next day, my co-worker asks me, with a panicked expression and an explosive tone, if I might have seen the sheet with graphic x on it.

In conversation, it turns out that it is very possible that he crumpled up said sheet and threw it on the floor....

So what is the moral of the story?

Every change I intend can bring one or more *additional* changes with it.

This happens with almost every change at all and not only with the ones I intend.

Every event and thus every action does not take place in isolation in a vacuum, but affects several different levels.

This is due to the interconnectivity - the being connected with each other - of all parts of our physical universe.

So, every time I want to change something consciously, it can't hurt to have a broad or broader consciousness than before about which radius of effect the change I primarily intend can have or even has.

Such awareness can enable me on the one hand to be careful and to avoid unpleasant or unwanted things.

On the other this way I can act in a more targeted, change-intelligent or even multi-layered way

and therefore I can be for example more multi-ef-
fective or time-efficient.

6. The Roots Of Life Intelligence

Change-intelligent awareness is one of the most effective prerequisites for learning-intelligent action and thus for more effective life control.

Learning actions can have a primarily additive (I'm learning to ride a bike), primarily subtractive (I'm quitting smoking), or primarily transformative (I'm learning to listen better) effect and bring about results, that are (1) undesirable (I'm exhausted and know little compared to the learning time I've invested because I haven't allowed myself recovery breaks) or (2) multi-faceted in a beneficial way (I'm learning a new dance and also learning to listen better: My partner and the dance instructor). Or I use the breaks during my learning work in such a way that I am physically active: either in the park or in my own space. Thus I recover mentally and at the same time increase my general physical well-being). Breaks do not always have to mean doing nothing; sometimes, however, doing nothing and letting go completely are just the right thing to do.

As beings who are constantly changing, in a world that is constantly changing, we are learning all the time one way or another. Just by the fact that our feeling, perceiving and thinking are incessantly confronted with new things, even when we are not active, we go through new experiences that leave unprecedented living information in us. This information can change both our knowledge and our skills. And learning is change of knowledge and skill through experience: additive, subtractive, or transformative.

It makes sense, before we decide what to learn and how to live, that we extensively observe and understand ever more deeply the movement of reality or the flow of change in its many different varieties. Thus (a) we nourish the roots of a living intelligence for learning, acting and living, through which (b) we fulfill one of the strongest prerequisites for a successful life. By participating in the change of reality that is always already taking place.

Part II:

Conscious Living

7. Reality And Transformation

One of the most important conditions for our well-being is the feeling and state of self-control. This means that in the midst of the multi-layered becoming that we are and the multi-layered becoming that surrounds us and in which we participate at the same time, we need the feeling that what we experience and feelingly perceive or what happens to us must either be chosen or accepted by us.

Something that we experience or that happens to us can or is only chosen or accepted by us if it resonates with our respective state of being. We can only accept something new if it does us good or at least promises us something good and is not threatening.

At the same time, we cannot always know or decide in advance what the effect of new things will be on us. Thus, we often allow types of happenings that promise us something good at the first moment, but later turn out to be threatening or critical to our well-being to some degree.

In a world that is not just our own or self-chosen playground, a breadth and width and height and depth of knowledge and skill are required. Thus we are empowered both to – even if always relatively – responsibly manage the many possible kinds of the threatening New, and to embrace and integrate the kinds of New that are essential to the inherent and unstoppable potential for growth or change that is within us....

Learning is the process in which we, as a living organism, come into contact with life contents that change according to the laws of nature, interact with them and are thereby transformed. The types or forms of this transformation we usually call change, knowledge acquisition, growth, transformation.

The knowledge about the totality of possibilities we have to handle or control the change and learning process that transforms us as well as possible, I call learning cybernetic.

8. What Is Cybernetics?

The term 'cybernetics' was introduced in 1948 by Norbert Wiener in "Cybernetics or Control and Communication in the Animal and the Machine".

Nowadays, cybernetics is understood as the science that studies the functioning and self-regulation of complex systems.

The active principle of self-regulating complex systems is that of navigation, which is also the literal translation of 'cybernetics'.

But the central question for a deeper understanding of cybernetics, I believe, concerns the purpose, goal, direction, and nature of navigation or control.

What is the purpose of steering and navigating?

To get where and how?

To achieve what?

To be in what or as what?

The answer is hidden in the concept of homeostasis (equilibrium).

Nowadays there are many technical constructions which are responsible for the maintenance of certain circumstances or states, such as air-conditioning systems or electricity supply systems.

They are responsible for a homeostatic standard, i.e. that they automatically bring back the temperature to this (same) level, if it should deviate from a certain level or standard.

As long as their functionality remains intact, these constructions ensure an automated self-regulation of a set state; in this respect they are cybernetic systems.

Further examples of cybernetic systems? The totality of all energy, the entire universe, the entire system physical forces, the terrestrial nature, the weather, the Earth's ecosystem, all living organisms, the human being, all human organs, all human energetic communication systems, the human brain, the human psyche. And of course much more...

Why do I call all these systems 'cybernetic'? What is their common cybernetic core? A homeostatically or equilibrically controlled movement or change - in the ocean or space of reality.

9. Basics Of Life Cybernetics

If I navigate an airplane from A to B, I apply aeronautical cybernetic knowledge.

If I do the same with a ship, then I apply nautical, maritime cybernetic knowledge.

If I navigate a spaceship, then I do astronautics, space cybernetics.

In all these cases I control the movement of an object from a certain space coordinate point to another. In other words, I am doing cybernetics of the movement of different means of transport - the Greek verb 'κυβερνώ' (kyberno), from which 'cybernetics' is derived, means to steer.

So in all these cases I bring - i.e. I steer and direct in a controlled way the movement of - something from place A to place B. The cybernetic knowledge or cybernetics applied in this process is needed for the safe reaching of the place B.

So first (1) I trace a line in space so that I can move from its beginning to its end, and then (2) I do so in a way that is safe, i.e. that not only ensures my survival, but also ensures the constancy of direction to the goal with the highest possible minimization of a risk of deviation. The safety of this way consists, as already mentioned above, in the maintenance of a homeostasis or equilibrium, an equilibrium.

Learning means change of knowledge and therefore change of being. In learning, I change my being, a certain so-being, by changing my knowledge, the to-something-enabling living information therefore, which I am.

The learning process is a happening, a "flow" of change. The learning process "flows" from one state to another. It happens anyway, i.e. very often (not always) in a natural and unconscious way, and it can also happen consciously; in addition possibly even voluntarily and actively.

If I now (consciously) have a learning goal and want to arrive there reliably, reach it reliably, and in such a way that I do not get out of balance - and possibly out of my path - I have to proceed in a learning cybernetic way. Learning something *safely* while *staying or being in balance* is therefore learning cybernetic action, applied learning cybernetics.

If I have a suitable life knowledge by learning and life experience, in order to maintain parts of my life as well as to reach new - smaller or larger - life goals, then I apply this life knowledge and act. By my acting and also my way of being I steer the happening in such a way that my life reality is maintained as well as new life goals are reached. Such controlling of life by acting and being I call life cybernetics.

Is that all? Yes. The much more important question is: What does it all mean exactly?

What exactly does balance mean? What exactly means safe? And even more: what all is involved in the acting and being that we call learning and living? Answering all of this is what makes learning and life cybernetics possible in the first place. So let's take a closer look into these key learning and life cybernetic aspects....

10. True Wanting

Cybernetic or control-intelligent action begins at – is fed from the very beginning by – the source of our true wanting.

Our will and our wanting is only true and not merely thought, if it is grounded in the "nerve cells" of our psychological-emotional nourishment and is initiated, permeated and dynamized by it.

This wanting is not explicitly, not specifically mentioned in the definition of 'cybernetics' - if cybernetics is the equilibric, i.e. balance-maintaining control of the safe direction of an initiated process - yet it is not only a part of it, but its literal soul, for it constitutes the moving force of cybernetic action.

Indeed, if I am to steer towards a direction, that direction is decided both by my present location or state and by the goal or purpose to be achieved.

A direction or the meaningfulness of action cannot be determined without a goal or a corresponding purpose.

The purpose now or the aim of a movement is

determined by a cause or a reason. This reason, as far as human beings are concerned, arises always through a need; through a wanting.

As far as this wanting is concerned, it is not always sufficient for an action to be activated. Therefore, every action and every movement are set in motion and maintained by a sufficiently strong wanting. The truer, i.e. more real this wanting is, the more effective will be the action driven by it.

And how are we to recognize the degree of reality of our wanting? The criterion for this I call significance.

Significant, substantial, or important learning or action takes place when it is driven by meaningfulness, that is, by what is personally significant. And meaningful is what we – as an *organismic wholeness* – *need* in a given moment or stage of life.

True wanting is recognized by the fact that what is wanted is personally significant, important to us. The degree of reality of our wanting is therefore determined by the degree of importance of what is wanted.

How high this degree is, can be different, but for a true wanting it must be at least sufficient; and that insofar as the unfulfillment of what is wanted

"There is a difference between goal and goal. One time the goal lies in the activity itself, the other time still besides the activity in some object to be brought forth by it. But where another goal is striven for besides the activity, the work to be produced for this purpose is naturally of higher value than the activity itself."

Aristotle

causes an inner and sufficiently disturbing restlessness. If this is given, we can proceed to the second
learning and life cybernetic key.

11. Goals As Manifestations Of Love

Let us suppose that we want to behave more ecologically correct; or we want to become more emotionally intelligent.

While both of these goals are (generally speaking) interpersonal, and therefore also politically and socially "correct," they are actually only illusory or unreal if they are pursued, let alone realized, for mere reasons of reasonableness. Why? Because then they do not cause any or no considerable unrest or restlessness in our inner being. Of course, there is always a certain power in reasons of reasonableness, every reason has that in itself in any case. The question is only, how strong a force is out of reasonableness and how much it causes in the end.

What should we be concerned about if we did not achieve the goals of ecological correctness or emotional intelligence as long as there was no suffering involved or the absence of a correspondingly satisfying state did not hurt us?

Further, ecological correctness may be initiated

out of a need for political adrenaline activism or an economically cosmetic measure. Similarly, emotional intelligence could be motivated out of a quest for a manipulative know-how.

If, for example, ecological correctness - or emotional intelligence - are goals, it must first be clear what they mean, i.e. what inner need they ultimately nourish, and then this need must affect or touch us in such a way that we emotionally need its fulfillment, because it is only through such fulfillment or nourishment that we truly feel good. Thus goal and motivation coincide; for both are in truth manifestations of love.

A goal, and therefore a learning goal or life goal, is not properly determined when the right motivation is sought or even created for a chosen goal, but when it *is* an authentic manifestation of an *already existing* true motivation. And a true motivation moves us insofar as it brings us closer to a state in which or as which *we want to be*.

Every goal has its roots in something that has the power to create or maintain a nurturing state within us.

Nourishment, in all its physical, mental-emotional and spiritual dimensions, is the key to a contented and genuinely free life.

A walk in the forest is a self-nourishing activity. Driving from the city to a forest with a forest walk as a destination, is a means to that end. Maintaining forests at all, in turn, is both a means with the goal of securing existentially necessary basics and an act out of love for nature and all living things.

Everything that is necessary for the sustainment of *aliveness* at all is the one dimension of nourishment.

And everything that permeates and imbues this aliveness with the chemistry and physics of *love* is the other dimension of nourishment.

Without these dimensions of nourishment, all meaning and motivation is absent.

Both of these dimensions are manifestations and expressions of the (it)self-desiring *in-love* state. When both are present, everything is there.

12. Life Intelligent Being And Acting

A true life goal, which would be a life goal that corresponds to our *felt* and *not merely imagined* organismicity and aliveness, must satisfy our natural urge for nourishment; rather: it should represent the fulfillment of this urge insofar as this fulfillment satisfies one or more of our needs.

If this is given, a life cybernetics, i.e. an intelligent life control becomes possible:

A. True wanting ensures life-controlling equilibrium.

This is because true wanting is a powerful star that exists in the space of our mind and soul.

Such wanting acts as an unshakable gravitational attractor that holds all of our corresponding activities in alignment and keeps us - in our fundamental state - in equilibrium.

In this equilibrium, we are clear, reliable and unwavering because the alignment of our forces is rooted in the lush soil of natural self-love.

B. A right goal secures the direction of events and processes through the correspondingly dynamized action and being.

A life goal is nothing more than the fulfillment-expression of a need.

A life goal is nothing more than the fulfilling expression of a need. Through acting and being, knowledge and skills are to be internalized and acquired, which quantitatively and qualitatively reshape or reconfigure our entire being and suchness.

The more personally significant the aspired life goal is, the more balanced and purposeful the entire corresponding acting and being will be.

C. Successful action consists in the conscious execution of life cybernetic acts.

Even if action also takes place unconsciously, we can control only the conscious action and partly the general and concrete life context or certain situations in which unconscious action and being take place.

And we can control the conscious action by being conscious, alert, attentive and nourished with-emotional-power.

Life cybernetic action always extends in a *peri-*

od of time, which is needed until a corresponding life goal is reached.

On this time axis, motivational clarity, a thorough goal definition, and a strategy that is both well thought-out and alive are the necessary components; but from its beginning, throughout acting and being, and until the life goal is reached, there must indeed always be a *repetitive* action or process, *continuously* or in *successive* steps.

Such action or process involves every single time and on different levels simultaneously a series of psychological, physical and cognitive *acts* or *steps*.

These acts or steps of directed action and experiential being are the most important states, qualities, skills and activities of human life; especially when it comes to sufficient or substantial or fairly deep *life mastery*.

These acts or steps of directed action and experiential being, these **master acts of life**, namely **feeling**, **wanting**, **knowing**, **deciding**, **learning** and **mastering**, are what the next and third part of the book is about.

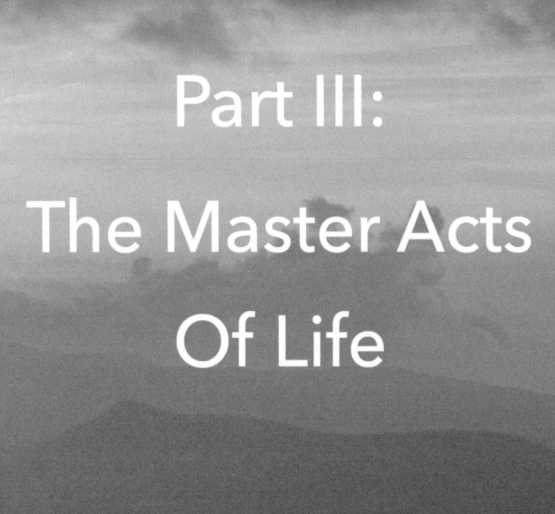

Part III:

The Master Acts
Of Life

13.

About Feeling

1

As *psychophysical* beings, we are a *complex energetic* happening.

1.1

The fact that we are psychophysical is *given*. We did not decide it, we cannot change it, we *are* it.

1.2

Our psychophysicality is a threefold complexity; it consists of three components.

1.3

We are psychic beings, so *mental-emotional* and *spiritual* experience is possible to us, and we are physical beings, that is, we are able to experience and live through a certain range of *physical* or *bodily* experiences.

1.4

The physical, the mental-emotional and the spiritual differ energetically in that they have different *degrees* of energetic *condensation*. They are different degrees of condensed energy manifestations.

1.41

Physical events "move" within a continuum between a relatively gross material and a relatively subtle energy condensation.

1.42

Mental-emotional-spiritual events "move" within a continuum of subtle energy happening, which has most different degrees of quality and intensity.

1.43

Mental events "move" within a continuum of subtle energy, which is fed by representations and abstractions, which are created by our physical and mental interaction with the inner and outer world and environment.

1.51

Under normal circumstances, it is rare, but not impossible, to experience something that does *not* activate or involve physical, mental, and spiritual components *simultaneously*.

1.52

Moreover, the three components of our psychophysicality are in mutual interaction with each other.

2

As part of conditional reality, we are *both depen-dent* and *"independent"* of it.

2.1

As a *part* of the total energy of the conditional reali-ty, our psychophysicality is an energetic happening, i.e. an energy *process*, a continuous energy *move-ment* therefore, *within the total* energy movement of the conditional reality.

2.2

As an *energetic part* of the total energy of the con-ditional reality, we are *dependent* on it.

2.21

We *cannot* exist without food, water, oxygen.

2.22

We often find it difficult to exist without at least some *emotional* meaningfulness and nourishment.

2.23

Last but not least, we depend on the laws of the whole nature and reality as well as specifically of our planetary nature and reality to *remain stable*.

2.3

Within this energetic dependence, we are "independent" to a *relative* degree.

2.31

"Independent" we are *in the* sense that within a gigantic universal interdependence, (1) we are a form that is self-enclosed to a relative degree, and (2) we have a limited *ability and freedom* of movement, decision and action.

2.311

We can form, unfold, create, control, decide, experience in many different ways.

3

As psychophysical beings we get more or less "disturbed" by the totality of "our" conditional reality. We notice *only a part* of this "disturbing". We call this noticing sensing or *'feeling'*.

3.1

The energy movement that constitutes our psycho-physicality 'dwells' or unfolds *more* or *less freely* or *unhindered* within the total energy movement of conditional reality, depending on conditions and circumstances.

3.2

Already in the first moment of the smallest obstruction of our psychophysical energy totality in its homeostatic (constant) dwelling or unfolding an *energetic disturbance* arises.

3.3

The causes of this obstruction or energetic disturbance can lie both inside and outside our psychophysicality.

3.4

From the totality of all possible energetic disturbance causes within and outside of our psychophysicality, countless disturbance possibilities arise.

3.5

Many of these disturbance possibilities remain
completely or partially unnoticed.

3.6

Others are noticed more or less clearly, but not always *to the same degree of transparency*.

3.7

The noticing of all *noticeable* energetic disturbances of our psychophysicality we call sensing or 'feeling'.

4

Feeling is the *"synapse"* of our consciousness to the totality of perceptible conditional reality.

4.11

A certain part of the energetic happening that constitutes the totality of our psychophysicality stands out from the rest of the energetic happening as a vibrating field.

4.111

This vibrating field functions as an *existence illuminating* space.

4.12

That which is within this energy field or space is existentially illuminated.

4.121

When something is existentially illuminated within this vibrating energy field, then it can be perceived in the facticity (actuality) of its *being there*.

4.21

In being *able to be perceived*, something can be

known.

4.22

The energy field or space in which the being-there of something *can* be perceived, we call 'field-of-being-conscious'.

4.3

The becoming-conscious or knowing of the being-there of something we call 'the *being-conscious-of-it*'.

4.4

The becoming-conscious or knowing of the being-there-of something within the field of consciousness takes place when by means of sentient carriers an energetic *directedness* towards this something arises, which we call the 'subject-object dichotomy'.

4.401

A sentient carrier is a *subsystem* of our total psycho-physical energy event.

4.402

This subsystem *is able* to be excited by contact with

"Through organismic sensing, each person becomes able to allow his whole organism, while engaging his conscious thinking, to weigh and balance each stimulus, need and desire as well as its relative weight and intensity. This complex weighing and balancing enables him to discover the line of action that comes closest to satisfying all his long-term and immediate needs in the given situation."

Carl R. Rogers

different stimuli (parts) of our total conditional reality.

4.403

Then it transmits the effect of this excitability and
lets it have an effect in the total psychophysical energy event, which constitutes us.

4.41

Such sentient carriers are the psychophysical systems, which are responsible for seeing, hearing or
feeling, for example.

4.42

The arousal of sentient carriers within the field of
consciousness by an external or internal stimulus
causes a *focusing process* to occur within the field
of consciousness.

4.421

Each focus is the bringing together of something *to
a particular point*.

4.422

The directedness of focused consciousness we also

call *'attention'*.

4.43

The focalization arising in the field of consciousness we call the 'subject-object dichotomy'.

4.431

The object is that which is *projected* at the *focal point* of the focusing - the energetic directionality that has arisen.

4.432

And subject is the space of consciousness in which an object is projected or appears.

4.5

The bipolar event by which a subject becomes aware - and therefore cognizant - of an object in its identity in a more or less concrete way is what we call 'perceiving'.

4.6

The act of perceiving is only the end or final stage of a multistage process. The stages of this process are the following:

4.61

Conditional Reality.

4.62

Psychophysicality.

4.63

Field of consciousness.

4.64

Psychophysical subsystems (sentient carriers: our senses for example).

4.65

Parts of conditional reality (stimuli).

4.66

Arousal of sensitive carriers by stimuli.

4.67

Focusing of consciousness (attention).

4.68

Emergence of the subject-object dichotomy; which enables the act of perception.

4.69

Perceiving (recognizing the identity of) an object.

4.7

The central role in this multilevel process is played by the contact point through which parts of conditional reality can enter our consciousness.

4.71

Through this contact point, our consciousness can come into contact with certain contents of conditional reality.

4.8

However, not everything (all stimuli) that excites or arouses our sensitive carriers (e.g. our senses) is illuminated or perceived by our attention; but only that which is selected by the inter"play" of our respective strongest needs of our psychophysicality and attracts the focus of our consciousness as a motivational attractor.

4.9

The act of experiencing something (4.431) as a subject (4.432), when we direct our focus of consciousness to a part of what is previously present through the arousal of our sentient carriers from parts of our conditional reality, we call sensing or *'feeling'*.

4.10

Feeling is therefore the *'synapse'* and *point of contact* and thus the *opening* of our consciousness to the totality of perceptible conditional reality.

5

'Living' means feeling and 'feeling' means *being touched.*

5.01

Our consciousness *can* focus on everything that arises from the arousal of our sentient carriers.

5.02

The direction of the focusing of our consciousness is decided by the respective activated motivational attractors.

5.11

What our consciousness does not focus on, is *not sensed or felt*, and therefore *not experienced*.

5.12

'Experiencing' or 'living' means *sensing* or *feeling*.

5.2

If sensing or feeling could be compared to a sense, it would be the sense of touch.

5.21

The core of the sense of touch is contact; or touch.

5.22

Touch as a basic event is the basis of all senses, all sensing, all feeling.

5.3

Sensing or feeling is the touching of "the skin" or the contact surface or contact *space* of our consciousness from conditional reality.

5.31

Everything that we *experience* and *can* experience results from *this touch*.

6

The *quality* of our life is determined by the quality *and* quantity of *our feeling*.

6.1

Our whole life consists *of and in what we feel*.

6.11

Physical and sensual sensing is feeling, mental sensing is feeling, mental "feeling" and experiencing is feeling.

6.12

Even more: instinct is feeling, intuition is feeling.

6.13

Even the most subtle state is not possible without feeling or sensing, that is, without any contact of any energy with the space that opens and sustains itself through our present consciousness.

6.14

Conscious psychophysical being *as a whole* is a feeling existence and being.

6.15

And *psychophysical consciousness in itself* is also *pure* feeling.

6.2

Compared to all the organismic inherent capacities available to us, sensing is the *most catalyzing*, *transforming*, *nurturing* and *healing*.

6.21

And it *can* be that especially when we have the *knowledge* of what we *"should"* feel and under what *conditions*.

7

Our feeling ability - and thus the *"richness"* of our life - widens and deepens in the space, which is *free of reaction*.

7.11

Against the background of the assumption or the *fact* that authenticity - as the quality of the real - is the only true answer to the need for fullness of being and life, the *feeling capacity* is our only true access to it.

7.12

What *normally* hinders a fullness of being and life is an unnatural hypnosis that *stifles* the spontaneous.

7.13

"Unhealthy" because *unnatural* and *hypnotically* originated incrustations and reaction patterns melt and dissolve when the avoidance reasons that led to them are *felt*.

7.21

'To be felt' means to be *allowed* as a *psychophysical* happening - along with all its associated roots

- within a *relaxed* and *freely* focused consciousness.

7.22

Once unnatural and hypnotically created incrustations and reaction patterns have dissolved, our consciousness awakens from the hypnosis of the inauthentic and begins to *coincide* tracelessly with what happens spontaneously.

7.23

Then our sensing and feeling capacity begins to deepen and expand without limits. This is *stepping into fullness*.

14.

About Wanting

1

As *psychophysical* beings we are *never* in the state of absolute equilibrium.

1.1

'Psychophysical' means first of all that we are a part of material *physis* (=nature). We experience ourselves as a totality of *physical* energy forms.

1.2

In addition, we experience ourselves as *psyche*, i.e. as a totality of soul, mind and spirit. We experience *emotions*, i.e. feeling energy forms, and *cognitive* perceptions and states, i.e. mental energy forms.

1.3

To *what extent* we-as-*psyche* exist ultimately as a result of something material is not dealt with in the present context.

1.4

As psychophysicality, i.e. as a totality of body energy, emotion and cognition, we are completely a complex energetic event.

1.5

An energetic happening is subject to - or is equivalent to - the first law of conditional reality: the law of *motion*.

1.51

As an energetic happening we are therefore *primarily* movement and therefore (at the same time) also *change*.

1.52

Even if we experience ourselves as a person with constant *identity*, energetically we are in *constant* change.

1.61

As a psychophysicality or... as *energy*, we are de facto a movement event. This fact implies that we are *never* in absolute equilibrium, i.e. absolute motionlessness.

1.611

By 'equilibrium' I mean (here) the state of being in a *balanced* state of rest.

1.62

Also during a meditative state of experienced-"absolute" rest or during deep sleep we are (physically and organismically) perpetual *change*.

2

As full participants in the cyclic rhythm of change of conditional reality, we "develop" states of lack. These we call *needs*.

2.11

As an energetic-psychophysical being, we are a perpetual process of change. As such we are a totality of *different* and simultaneously *parallel* changes.

2.12

The mode of change of *conditional* reality exhibits a *rhythmic* character.

2.121

'Conditional' or '*dependent*' is here to be understood as opposed to 'absolute' or '*independent*'.

2.13

The essence of this rhythm is the *cycle*: day and night, ebb and flow, star birth and star death. Concerning us humans: hunger and satiety, tiredness and energeticness, excitement and boredom, interest and repulsion. These are only a *few* examples.

2.2

Our existence and being alive is part of an energetically never ending cycle of a recurring alternation of opposites.

2.21

The structure of this cycle is always the same:
Coming into being > Changing > Passing away.

2.3

We are in *no* moment of this cyclic happening in the state of absolute equilibrium.

2.31

Whether in the physical or mental realm, we are always in the cyclic alternating process of *moving* from one state of change to another.

2.4

Our natural life impulse urges the energy event that we are to its equilibrium, that is, to a state of rest and peace; to a state of contentment.

2.41

This impulse is existentially *"innate"* or given to us

by our human nature and reality.

2.5

By the *coming together* of our impulse to satisfaction with the - due to the laws of reality - *psychophysically never* attainable state of the absolute equilibrium, the feeling constantly arises in us that something is *missing*.

2.51

When something in us is missing, it keeps us *away* from the absolute equilibrium. The state of rest then is disturbed.

2.52

To the *feeling* of this state of lack I give the name 'need'.

2.53

In the state of lack, we *need* the thing that we lack.

2.531

In other words, what we lack is needed by us.

2.54

When we *lack* a thing, this thing needs to be *found* and *absorbed* by us.

3

We perceive some needs as *self*-activated and fully *justified* and some as *externally* activated and merely *necessary*. Both are true because we *cannot deny* them without unpleasant consequences.

3.1

The *first* sensation (*feeling of something...*) of a need, i.e. a state of lack, is initially *source*-blind.

3.11

This means that in the moment of origin of the sensation of a need we do *not know*, i.e. we are not *aware*, what is the reason, cause or origin of this sensation.

3.2

Once we have identified this sensation or need in its distinctive uniqueness through our perceptual and cognitive faculty, we find ourselves in a position to "sense" both its origin (e.g. a dryness or lack of water) and its fulfillment or satisfaction (e.g. a supply of water). This is the *second* sensing, which is more equivalent to 'perceiving'.

3.21

This *second* sensing (*sensing something <u>as</u>*...) of a need opens the basis for us to find out whether the need we sense has its origin *"in"* or *"outside"* us.

3.3

A need originating *"within"* us, that is, *without* the influence of external necessities or compulsions, we call *endogenous* (born within) or *self*-activated.

3.4

A need originating *"outside"* us, i.e. *by* influence of external necessities or constraints, we call *exogenous* (born outside) or *externally* activated.

3.5

Both self-activated and externally activated needs are true, because in *both* cases we are in a state of deficiency.

3.6

Certainly, an *intrinsically*-activated, and therefore fully justified need is automatically and *naturally* assumed by us, because it concerns us *directly*.

"Every being has a possibility to unfold that is given to it. Carl Rogers calls this "actualization tendency". It wants to be sensed and thus known. It takes place in a self-directedness that aims at self-unfolding and development. The actualization tendency contains an "implicit knowledge". This implicit knowledge is a biological-genetic, spiritual and holistic fact given by reality."

Inghard Langer

3.7

An *externally*-activated, and therefore perceived by us as merely *necessary*, need is *not* naturally assumed because it concerns us *indirectly*.

3.8

Externally activated needs are not *felt* to be fully justified because in the case of absolute *freedom* we would *not* like to feel them.

3.81

We recognize externally activated needs as partially *justified* because they arise in *our* life world and through the laws of *reality*.

3.9

To some extent we already have the freedom to change the circumstances in and the conditions of the life-world in which we exist by our influence. The laws of reality, however, we cannot change.

3.10

The more authentically and completely we feel and therefore observe the laws of reality, the more likely it is that an externally activated or exogenous need can be felt by us as self-activated or endogenous.

4

Every true need *pushes* us to fulfill it. This leads to the feeling of *restlessness*. *Feeling* this restlessness leads us to the state of *being motivated*.

4.1

It is a psychophysical law that every true need of a living organism urges or even compels that organism to move.

4.11

The emergence of a need, i.e. the disturbance of our relative equilibrium, is at the same time the emergence of a motive force and thus the generation of a *movement*.

4.12

Every movement has a goal or a destination or a target.

4.121

The movement out of a need, i.e. out of a lack (see 2.31-2.51), has as its goal the removal of the existing lack.

4.2

As long as we cannot or are not allowed to give in to the urge or compulsion to move in order to eliminate our equilibrium-disturbance, we feel *restlessness*.

4.21

This restlessness is the result of the conflict between the gravitation from the goal that holds the possibility of our perturbation removal and the circumstances, forces or reasons that prevent us from acting and moving toward that goal now.

4.3

We characterize this restlessness as 'directed toward a goal' or 'purposeful'.

4.4

This purposeful restlessness is a pregnant woman whose labor has begun. It is absolutely ready to show its true face *instantly*, namely *movement*.

4.41

This absolute readiness to move, which we feel *before* we *start* to move (Latin: movere), is an *ener-*

getic state. It is the state, then, of being *moved*-to-ward-something or of being *driven*-to-something or of being-*attracted*-to-something. We give this state the name *'motivatedness'* (medieval Latin: *motivus* = *causing movement*).

Perceived and *felt* motivatedness creates an *energy* field. This field acts as a center of *gravity* and a *fuel* tank at the same time. We give to the state in which we feel and are this energy field the name '*wanting*'.

5.1

As soon as a motivatedness to do something has arisen, a field is created in us in which energy - as potential or actual availability - accumulates.

5.11

This accumulated energy or power of transformation is fed by the programming of our psychophysical nature.

5.21

The resulting accumulation of energy functions as a field that can be experienced from two different perspectives:

5.22

gravitational or *magnetic* when we feel *attracted* to the goal of our motivations, or *impulsive* when we feel *driven* to that goal.

5.3

Regardless of whether the energy field is perceived as <u>gravitational or attracting-from</u> or <u>fuel-tank or driving-to</u>, in either case it generates the power source necessary to an action or mode of being.

5.31

We call the state in which we *feel this energy field* 'wanting'.

6

There is *true* wanting and there is *"pseudo"* wanting.

6.1

Not everything that is *called* 'wanting' *is* actually wanting.

6.2

Very often the state of *wishing* is called 'wanting'. But wishing is not wanting.

6.21

If one nevertheless wants to call the state of wishing 'wanting', one should add that this wanting is rather a kind of "Harry Potter" wanting.

6.22

When I feel a "Harry Potter" wanting, it means that I do want something (sometimes very much), but I don't want to *work* for it, I don't want to make an *effort* for it. I wish I had a "Harry Potter" wand with which I could instantly change the world so that I could have or be the something I want in this world.

6.221

The "Harry Potter" will is *devoid of drive*. It does not have the power to cause or initiate action.

6.3

True wanting, i.e. *real* wanting, *generates action*. I *cannot* feel it and remain *passive and inactive* at the same time.

6.31

We recognize true wanting by restlessness. (s. 4.2-4.4)

6.32

When I *really* want something, I *recognize* it by the fact that I become *restless* when *I do not yet have or am not yet in possession* of what I want. *So restless* that I *automatically* surrender to the urge to *move*, which generates the necessary *action* that leads me to what is *wanted*.

7

In order to recognize action-effective, i.e. true wanting, we need a *free sensing and feeling space* and an *awake consciousness*.

7.0

Nothing can be moved through action and attitude effectively that does not originate from a true need, regardless of whether this need is endogenous or exogenous.

7.1

If I am thirsty, I can know by my nature-given instinct what I need, i.e. water, and either act instantly or, as long as I do not act toward the goal of my need, I feel a growing restlessness.

7.2

If I am restless and do not know why, I need the circumstance of *freedom* in several ways, so that I can relax and my consciousness can become more awake, i.e. more capable of feeling.

15.

About Knowing

1

Energy is the *mysterious movedness of manifested fullness of being*.

1.1

The self-"luminous" or self-sustaining context or "space" of all and any existence is *absolute being*.

1.2

The absolute being is *not within* the range of human grasping or comprehending, but is identifiable only through *being* and by *most free* spontaneity.

1.3

The absolute being is not nothing, but *everything*.

1.4

The totality of everything includes both manifested and non-manifested existence and entities.

1.41

Non-manifest existence, however, is not nothingness, but free, i.e. unattached, unbound existence, which is *"unbearably" full of itself*.

1.411

In this "unbearable" and therefore vibrating fullness of non-manifested being a movedness emerges (does itself out) in mysterious way (without apparent and/or necessary reason).

1.412

This movedness is therefore the mysterious expression of the vibration of the absolute fullness of being.

1.413

This mysterious movedness of manifested fullness of being is *the free form* of what we humans call 'energy'.

1.5

'Energy' means *in work*, i.e. *in motion*, and *is* therefore a kind of *movedness*: the mysterious movedness of the manifested fullness of being.

2

Everything that exists in conditional, bound or manifested form is an energetic being-*in-form*; an energetic *in-form*-ation.

2.0

There is free, i.e. *non-bound*, energy, and there is *bound* energy.

2.1

Free energy binds itself by the vibratory force of absolute fullness of being in different degrees of condensation and by this process of condensation passes from its unconditionality, unboundness or formlessness to an infinite majority or number of conditional, bound or form-autonomous energetic existences.

2.2

Every *single* existent something is a quantity of energy which binds itself by the vibrational force of absolute fullness of being from the sea of energetic formlessness to a form-autonomous *singularity*, i.e. to a *form-like* and *singular* appearance or existence.

2.21

Each such singularized (energetically-bound) existence is thus a certain *in-formed* (and *previously* formless, free) quantity of energy.

2.3

The *being-in-form* of a singular existence brought forth from a certain energetic quantity we call *in-form-ation*.

2.4

An in-form-ation or (from now on) *information* is (thus) an energy *being-in-a-determined-form*.

2.41

Everything that exists *manifested* is therefore an (energetic) *information*.

2.42

An information is therefore *always* an energetic manifestation and *never* non-manifest. There is *no non*-energetic information.

3

As energetic manifestations, we humans also represent an *in-form*-ation. We are *energy brought into a certain form*.

3.0

The *in-form-ation* that *we* are is a complex system of a form-ness consisting of a complex totality of individual and interacting energy condensations.

3.11

There exist simple (atomic or monadic), i.e. (here) *not divisible* energetic kinds of information;

3.12

and many *more and more complex* (energetic) kinds of information.

3.2

Each more complex information consists of the interconnection of *simple* and/or *less complex* kinds of information with each other.

3.3

Each standing-together of simple and/or complex

kinds of information with each other is a *system* ('System' = standing together): an information-*complex*.

3.4
Within the continuum of more and more complex (energetic) kinds of information exist *lifeless* and *living* (energetic) systems or information-complexes.

3.5
Living systems differ from lifeless ones in that they have certain properties:

3.51
the property of *energy interaction* and *exchange*

3.511
between themselves-as-a-whole and their surrounding environment, and

3.512
between energy systems that are in themselves;

3.52
the property of inherent *reproductive capacity*; and

3.53

the property of *growth* (where growth here means not only *becoming more*, but the progression of a holistic becoming, or a complete realization of the inherent destiny of that becoming).

3.6

We are a living (energetic) system constituted in a certain way:

3.61

a dynamic construction consisting of a gigantic totality;

3.62

of singular and smaller or larger systems of human biocells and the relations between them.

3.7

We are a very large *dynamic* energetic system;

3.71

a complex of multiple kinds of energetic information arranged together to form a dynamic, vibrant whole.

3.8

This dynamism of a living energy system is what we call *organismicity*.

4

Knowledge is *living information* which *enables us for something.*

4.0

Within the continuum of increasingly complex (energetic) kinds of information, we humans exist as a *living* (energetic) system.

4.1

We are a *complex, multidimensional living information*

4.2

Within our realm as a human organismic "universe" there are many different organismic (sub)systems that have different properties and enable different functions.

4.21

Thus, some (sub)systems are responsible for purely physical processes, others for mental-emotional processes, and others for mental or cognitive processes.

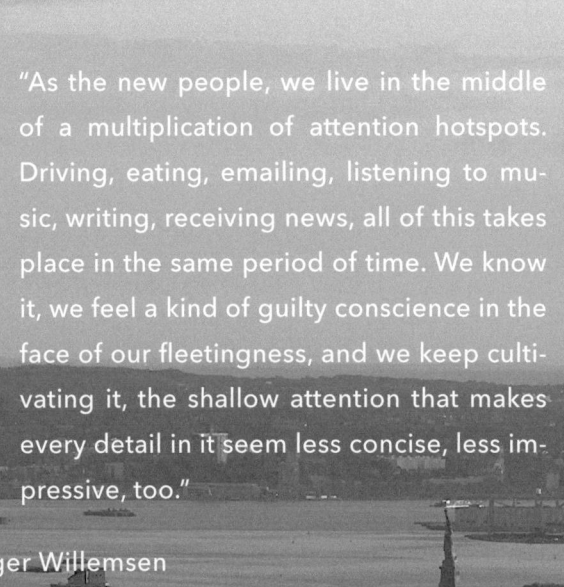

"As the new people, we live in the middle of a multiplication of attention hotspots. Driving, eating, emailing, listening to music, writing, receiving news, all of this takes place in the same period of time. We know it, we feel a kind of guilty conscience in the face of our fleetingness, and we keep cultivating it, the shallow attention that makes every detail in it seem less concise, less impressive, too."

Roger Willemsen

4.22

The *main purpose* of any single living information of one of our organismic (sub)systems is to *enable* another organismic building block or system to be *active* or *activated*.

4.3

This *to-something-enabling living information* I call *knowledge*.

4.31

In our totality, *we are* a total living information.

4.32

We *are* knowledge.

5

Knowledge change (or learning) occurs through participation in a relatively wide range of becoming. This can occur in two ways.

5.01

Since we are *knowledge* and are in *continuous, permanent change*, we can say that we are *permanent knowledge change*.

5.02

'Learning' I define as a *knowledge-changing process.*

5.03

From 5.01 and 5.02 it follows: We are, *as long as we live*, a learning happening, a learning process.

5.1

We learn, i.e. we change our knowledge by changing ourselves as *living information*.

5.11

Much of the learning process that we are is *passive* and *outside our conscious awareness*.

5.111

This applies to all the processes that are active in us due to our natural predispositions

5.112

and all processes which are activated and carried out *without our conscious knowledge* due to our contact with the conditions of the outside world.

5.113

The *innate* knowledge, therefore, that we are, *is* on the one hand (1) *there* from *the beginning* and on the other hand (2) *grows* through the unfolding and development of the inherent *destination and "destiny"* in us from the beginning.

5.1131

Both (1 and 2) occur both *intraorganismically* (*within* our total organismicity) and *transexorganismically* (through the relative receiving *permeability* of our organismicity to portions of the energetic information located in the *external world*).

5.12

Much of the learning that we are, however, can also

be *within* our conscious awareness and more or less *active*.

5.121

We call this kind of learning process *conscious* knowledge change.

5.1211

Conscious knowledge change can take place by merely *observing* the automoving (self-moving) learning process: in this way we get to see what change is taking place through our effortless participation in the becoming that is going on without our intervention.

5.1212

But conscious knowledge change can also take place by *actively* influencing our participation in the becoming that takes place without our intervention.

6

All knowledge change, i.e. all learning, takes place *when* an (energetic) information becomes *alive*. Knowledge is *always alive* and arises only *ontically*.

6.1

When something, i.e. an energetic information x, is *taken up and integrated* by us as an organismic whole or as a living information complex *in such a way that* it *transforms* us in our organismic totality *through* this information x, *then and only then* we call this information *living*, *then and only then* this information is *knowledge*.

6.2

If I hear today that Beijing is the capital of China, and later this information is *nowhere to be found within me*, it has *not* changed me-as-knowledge or me-as-living-information.

6.3

If it is later *findable*, then it has *changed* me (regardless of how long) and has therefore become a *living information*, because its existence either remains merely supported or maintained by my organismicity or because its existence has become inseparable from my organismicity.

6.4

In both cases it exists because *I am it* (see 4.32); by being *alive* and *containing* it;

6.41

therefore I call *all* knowledge *living* or *alive*;

6.42

therefore all knowledge arises *ontically* (through being); in that *we* transform it into a *part* of our living being or in that it transforms our living *being* by its *information content*.

6.5

Certainly, acquired knowledge, which is *lethargic*, is also possible: such knowledge is so asleep in my unconscious that I am *unaware* of its existence.

6.6

Furthermore, I call a knowledge <u>*confirmed by*</u> or <u>*consistent with*</u> reality

6.61

true knowledge or *gnosis* and a knowledge *not* yet
confirmed by reality and *only accepted* as true

6.62

faith or *pistis.*

7

The more a knowledge leads to the *realization of my actualization tendency*, the more *important* it is.

7.0

By what is decided whether the existence of an information which has become alive in me (and before was merely energetic) either remains *simply carried* or *maintained* by my organismicity or whether it even becomes *inseparable* from it (6.3)? There is a reason for it and two possibilities:

7.01

My transformation through this new information is embedded in a strongly emotional happening which took place *without* my decision.

7.02

My transformation through this new information is embedded in a strongly emotional happening that was *initiated* by *me*.

7.03

In both of these possibilities, then, *emotion* is the

key transformative initiator, catalyst, and shaper.

7.1

The weaker or stronger the emotion in a process that transforms my knowledge or me-as-knowledge, the weaker or stronger the corresponding knowledge or me-as-changed.

7.2

If I undergo a knowledge-changing and thus also a being-changing transformation through a process that I initiated myself, my transformation is the more important, the stronger it is triggered by an emotion that is fed by a motivation or a need, which arises in the living-intelligent space of my actualization tendency. The actualization tendency is the inherent urge to unfold, realize, and be what is inherently within us as it is touched, nourished, and dynamized by natural law reality.

7.3

From this it follows that the ever deeper and more comprehensive *knowledge of my actualization tendency* is the *most important* knowledge for me.

7.31

For this, *authentic sensing* and *openness to experiencing reality* are necessary.

7.311

The *gain* from this is a still *unknown* but immeasurably *fulfilling* knowledge, i.e. *vibrant existence*.

16.

About Deciding

1

As psychophysical beings, we experience needs; "deficiency" states, that is, that seek fulfillment.

1.01

Psychophysical energy is a cyclic phenomenon and process that constantly alternates between being <u>supplied with</u> and <u>consuming</u> power.

1.011

These are both *"deficiency"* states.

1.0111

If I must be supplied with force, then this must happen because I *lack force*. The lack of power is a deficiency state.

1.0112

If I must consume force, then this must happen because I have a *surplus of force*. Because of this surplus, I am not energetically balanced. The absence of energetic balance is a state of deficiency.

1.1

In place of every state of deficiency must come (naturally) the state of fullness. Either by supply or by consumption.

1.2

Here begins the search for fulfillment.

1.3

The beginning of the search for fulfillment opens, excites and activates our entire perceptual capability.

1.31

Our perceptual capacity is (also, *but not only*) our search instrument and consists of the five senses, our entire inner feeling and our intuition capacity: of the *totality*, therefore, of our sensing, feeling being.

2

The realm in which we seek fulfillment with our perceptual capacity is the world that is opened up and accessible to us.

2.0

As psychophysical organisms, we participate *partially* in the totality of conditional psychophysical reality.

2.01

This means that *only a part of all possibilities* is available to our possibilities of experience and knowledge.

2.02

This happens because we are *limited* beings, just as every other psychophysical or conditional entity (existing energy-formedness or entity) is limited.

2.1

Our limited horizon of experience and knowledge implies that the *realm* in which we want to and can find what we need to fulfill our needs is also limited.

2.11

Thus, there is a *limitation* to the possibilities of fulfilling our needs.

2.2

However, this limitation is not always automatically given, but results from the *combination of* (a) <u>the objective limitation of all possibilities</u> *with* (b) <u>the temporally respective state of our experience and knowledge horizon of all possibilities</u> *and* (c) <u>the spatiotemporally available range within the total range of all possibilities.</u>

2.21

If, for example, I am thirsty and neither water nor any other drink is available to me, the success of the fulfillment search of my thirst-quenching need will depend on (b) my *knowledge* of all *edible* and *water*-containing substances (fruits etc.), combined with (a) the totality of all *available* possibilities in this respect and (c) my spatiotemporal *location*.

2.211

For example, it is of no use to me if I know a water-containing plant that *is not present* in the radius of my "current" spatiotemporal location....

2.3

Thus, my chances of success (in fulfilling needs) increase by gaining greater knowledge and expanding spatiotemporal accessibility.

2.31

So even if it is difficult or impossible to know *all* the fulfillment possibilities of our needs, it is always possible to *multiply* these possibilities by expanding our horizon of experience and knowledge.

3

In a circumstance of sufficient or multiple possibilities of fulfillment of a need or necessity, the possibility of choosing opens up to us.

3.1

The success of the fulfillment of our needs can be fortunate or unfortunate.

3.11

This can depend on the actually available possibilities of fulfillment as well as on the actual development of all *preconditions* decisive for the success of fulfillment.

3.12

One of these preconditions is *the* or *a right choice*. What is meant by this?

3.2

At the moment when more than one possibility of fulfilling one of our needs or a pressing necessity, we have to *find out* whether and how the available possibilities would satisfy our need or fulfill the pressing necessity.

3.21

If I am thirsty, have nothing drinkable with me, but there is a water fountain nearby, then I would have to think *little*, i.e. *not at all*, about what to do.

3.22

However, if I have enough money with me, and there is also a kiosk next to the fountain with a certain selection of drinks, I can or will *think about* what would be the right or more beneficial *choice* for me.

3.23

Depending on the situation in life and the particular circumstances present, sometimes we have the *freedom* to make a choice, but in other cases we are *forced* to make a choice.

3.231

Having the freedom of choice, and always increasing that freedom, is a good compass for a more fulfilling life.

3.232

In the same way, it is of no small advantage to free ourselves from more and more of the existing constraints.

3.3

"To choose" means to decide for one of many fulfillment possibilities of a need or even another necessity. What does it mean 'to decide'?

4

(True) deciding means the act of (irrevocably) committing oneself.

4.1

'Decide' or 'to decide' means to *commit oneself* to one of several (of at least two) possibilities of fulfilling a need or necessity.

4.11

'To commit' oneself means to *irrevocably obligate oneself* now to a particular future way-of-being or -acting or -behaving.

4.111

'To obligate oneself' in the sense that the particular behavior, action, or being in the particular future time will no longer or may no longer be spontaneous or free, but as now determined.

4.112

'Irrevocable' in the sense that *acting now is already as decided*, or that it is a certainty and facticity that future behavior, acting, or being will be that which is *decided now*.

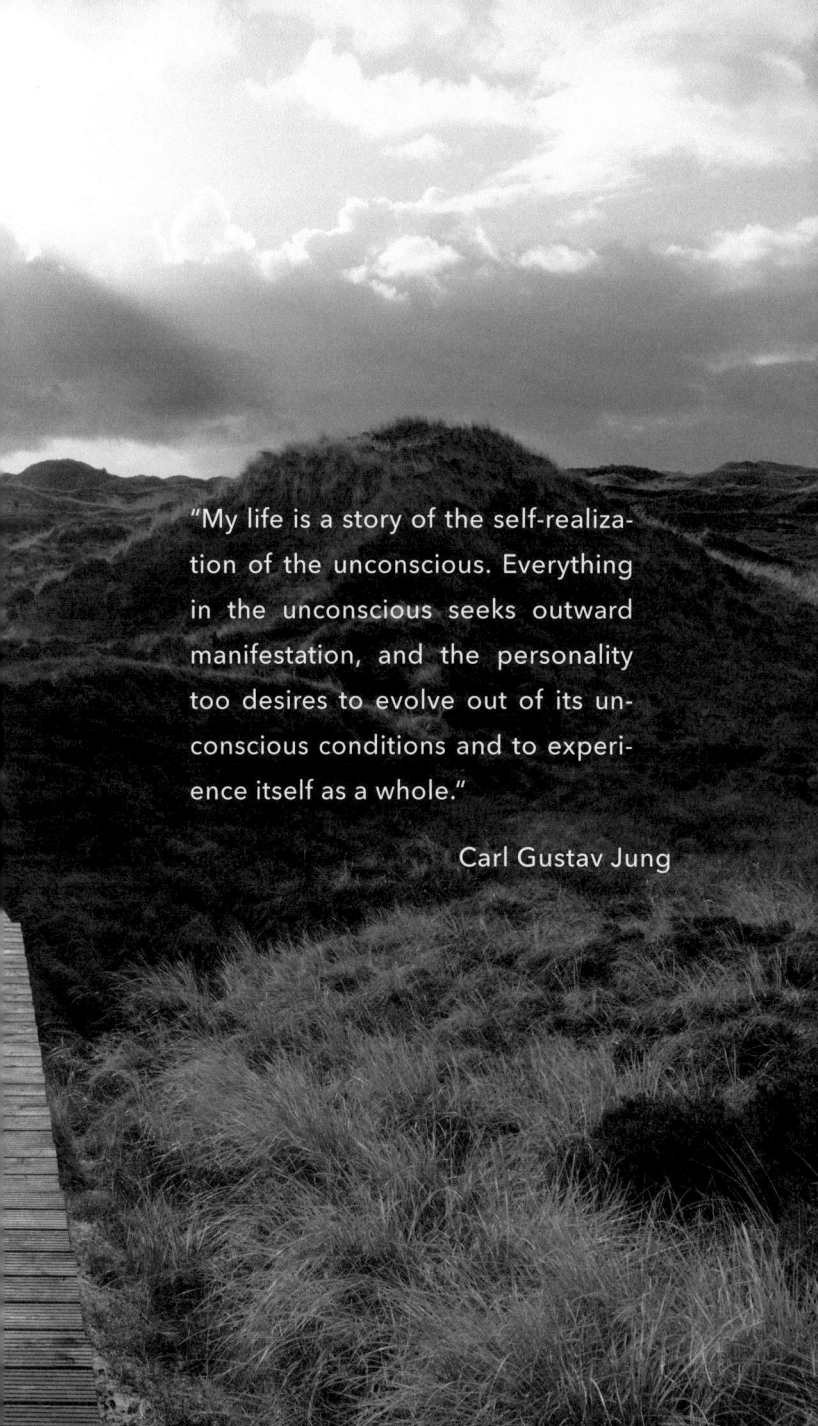

"My life is a story of the self-realization of the unconscious. Everything in the unconscious seeks outward manifestation, and the personality too desires to evolve out of its unconscious conditions and to experience itself as a whole."

Carl Gustav Jung

4.2

There are different situations in which it is necessary or important to make decisions.

4.21

Depending on the degree of necessity and importance of a decision, there are three varieties of decision-making.

5

There are the "luxurious", the meaningful and the existential decisions.

5.1

The "luxurious" decision is about "taste", about the "famous" icing on the cake or possibly about a post-modern neurosis.

5.11

What difference does it make whether I get chocolate or strawberry cream on my vanilla ice cream?

5.111

If I can't decide something like that spontaneously, I could flip a coin.

5.112

Nothing against empathizing with what one might like better. However, should it occupy one quite *seriously*, then it "smells" like neurosis.

5.12

Decision *errors* are *not threatening* or *serious* when making "luxurious" decisions.

5.13

But in the next two kinds of decision-making *they are*....

5.2

Meaningful decision-making is about choosing between mutually exclusive (rather, almost or completely) components that are important for the quality or/and *perpetuation* of our life in a certain respect.

5.21

If clearly different possibilities of being, behaving or acting *promise to change* my future life fundamentally

5.22

or in one of its relevant facets now strongly to the disadvantage, advantage or greater or greatest advantage,

5.23

then it *is meaningful* to *decide* the right one between these possibilities.

5.3

The more fundamentally or essentially a choice is about sustaining our life – whether in its physical, mental, or spiritual aspect – the more appropriate it is to speak of *existential* decision-making.

6

The instrumental "means" available to us to accomplish a decision are intuition and/or reason; they can "produce" the state of confidence and/or conviction needed to make a decision.

6.11

Even if the correctness of a decision act can only be shown *in the future*, a decision act must always be completed in the respective *present*, *independent* of a future success or failure.

6.12

In the (respectively present) completion of a decision, we rely in our decision-making *ability* both

6.121

on the ground of the past-saturated present and

6.122

on the projection of the (uncertainly) felt/imagined future.

6.2

Since decision-making always takes place with

regard to the future, which is uncertain, this decision-making (in the present) must take place both in a state of *confidence* and/or in the state of *conviction*.

6.21

To carry out a decision *in confidence* means that the consequences expected from this decision "will" occur because this corresponds to the laws of reality which are derived from our previous *subjective* and, for the most part, *unconscious-intuitive-successful* overall experience.

6.22

To carry out a decision *out of conviction* means that the consequences expected out of this decision "will" occur because this corresponds to the laws of reality which are derived from our previous *subjective* and, for the most part, *consciously-observationally-successful* overall experience.

6.3

The state of confidence arises from our *rather intuitive* perceptual faculty.

6.31

Intuition is the most subtle and therefore the freest form of sensing. It means feeling *into that which is closed to the grosser perceptive faculty.*

6.4

The state of conviction arises from our *more rational* perceptive faculty.

6.41

Intellect and/or reason is the faculty of *realizing, understanding, penetrating* and *judging* through what has been (so far in a more conscious way) experienced.

6.5

In the act of decision-making, intuition and reason are involved simultaneously.

6.6

A decision x for one of several different possibilities *takes place if* the totality of all (conscious and/or unconscious and all sensed and/or comprehended) reasons *for this one possibility x is therefore superior* to the totality of reasons for one or more other possibilities, because through *this possibility and decision x* the (at the time) greatest possible *degree of confidence* and/or *conviction* is achieved.

7

**The art of meaningful and existential deci-
sion-making consists in doing what an *intelligent spontaneity* clearly "tells" us; an intelligent
spontaneity, which is *grounded* in a continuously
more comprehensive *reality*.**

7.0

The more *complex* a given reality or situation is, the
more *challenging* our decision-making ability becomes.

7.01

This does not necessarily mean greater stress or
stress at all.

7.02

It just means that the *deeper* and *broader* the wisdom of our intuition and reason, the *easier* and
more confidently we will make a more complex decision.

7.03

The potential of deeper and further wisdom is tap-
pable in the *"infinity"* of the experiential universe.

7.11

The more *reality* (*coinciding* with the laws of reality) we experience and internalize in the experiential universe,

7.12

the deeper and wider the wisdom of our intuition and reason.

7.21

The deeper and wider the wisdom of our intuition and our reason,

7.22

the more comprehensive and intelligent our spontaneity of decision-making:

7.23

our ability, that is, to decide – by a present *total activation* of our feeling and knowledge –

7.3

a fulfillment possibility of a need or necessity;

7.31

a fulfillment possibility that is now more *reality-satu-*

rated than any other.

7.32

Because it is advisable to look for possibilities of fulfillment of needs or necessities which themselves are *also real* and not *illusionary*....

7.4

Blessed who can *answer*: What do I *really* <u>have</u> to decide?

17.

About Learning

1

We are a closed and at the same time open organismicity.

1.1

We are a living energetic system, which is composed of a multidimensional totality of energy condensations or energetic subsystems arranged with each other.

1.11

Such subsystems can be molecules, mitochondria, cells, organs and also functions, actions and states.

1.2

The dynamized nature of a living energy system is a characteristic property of its *organismicity*.

1.3

As dynamized living energetic systems, we are both a closed and an open organismicity.

1.31

We are a *closed* organismicity because the *functional* identity of the energetic arrangedness that we are is *relatively diachronic*, i.e. persists relatively through a given time.

1.32

We are an *open organismicity* because the *physical* - and therefore the *total psychophysical* - identity of the energetic arrangedness that we are is *relatively transforming*, i.e. perpetually relatively changing through a given time.

1.4

Also the becoming, to which we are "subject" from our birth to our death, is *closed*, because the conditional human reality is limited in several aspects by the natural laws, and *open*, because many different world-possibilities are open to the course and the existential expressivity of our being or "meet" it in one way or another....

The "clash" of our open organismicity with the "contents" of our energetic container brings about a series of "disturbances" or perturbations.

2.0

The characteristics that constitute a living system (like us) constitute the conditions of the possibility of an adjusting and conforming capacity; the capacity to adapt.

2.01

The adaptivity faculty consists not only in responding to external obstacles or disturbances after a previous passivity or activity,

2.02

but also in adapting to or changing in the direction of a self-chosen "reality" that does not yet exist.

2.03

The necessity of adaptation results from the simultaneous existence of:

2.031

(1) our relative well-being-through-the-equilibrium-state and

2.032

(2) our permanent energetic "being disturbed" by the reality "infinitely" penetrating and containing us.

2.11

This "getting disturbed" can be experienced relatively positively and/or relatively negatively or evaluated subjectively.

2.111

Negatively, hunger or emotional wounding can be experienced.

2.112

Positively, food or emotional nourishment can be experienced.

2.2

After each "getting and being disturbed" or a perturbation, our equilibric tendency automatically becomes active.

2.21

The equilibric tendency, or the inherent impulse to be in psychophysical equilibrium, in the state of equilibrium, is the motor of any of our unconscious or conscious activities. Through what?

3

Any sufficiently strong perturbation of our to-tal-organismic balance activates the process of equilibration.

3.1

Equilibrium is the state of total organismic balance. In it and as it, we are "motivationlessly" content; a tensionless-vibrant organismic flow; a psychophys-ically calm flow; a blissful synchronicity of change and continuity; of becoming and being.

3.2

This equilibrium is "disturbed" and disrupted for various reasons; i.e. natural and unnatural.

3.21

The equilibrium state with respect to our nourish-ment, for example, is that we are not hungry.

3.210

Now we may not be hungry at all, or only a little, or enough, or very much;

3.211

if we are *not* hungry *at all*, our equilibrial tendency does *not* yet trigger *any activation* in the direction of nourishment;

3.212

if we are a *little* hungry, it *gently awakens*;

3.213

if we are hungry enough, it has already moved us into an activated state, which is *energetically determined* and knows *no turning back*;

3.214

if we are *very* hungry, it transforms food into an irresistible *magnet* that *cannot be escaped*.

3.3

Whether hunger, emotional or differently psychophysical or mental neediness, boredom fighting, grief overcoming, confusion elimination, ecstasy "digestion" or other things "attack" our equilibrium, this will then trigger an action in the direction of its restoration, if the degree of disturbance of the respective perturbation exceeds our <u>psychophysical</u>

and <u>total energetic</u> tolerance.

3.4

We call the process of restoration of a disturbed equilibrium *equilibration*.

4

Over time, through the process of equilibration, we acquire those courses of action that stand the test of time.

4.1

The origin, nature and consistency of our needs always vary according to the combination and the mode of the coincidence or the interconnectedness

4.11

of our respective biological and psychophysical-mental-and-spiritual stages of development and growth, with

4.12

our respective reality system.

4.121

Our respective reality system is the respective spatiotemporal structuredness or arrangedness

4.1211

of all elements or entities or "contents" of our reality and

"We are never finished in the formation of our personality, but the dynamics of this process strongly decrease towards adulthood. It is even the case that adulthood is quite typically associated with this stabilization of the personality - it is said that a person has finally "found herself/himself"."

Gerhard Roth

4.1212

the totality of the relations between them.

4.2

Whatever the consistency of our needs, they always generate a motivational force for actions intended to serve their fulfillment and thus ensure the restoration of our psychophysical equilibrium.

4.3

Through our education, experience, and self-reflective development, we learn courses of action that fulfill our needs and those that do not or cannot.

4.4

We adopt the successful forms and patterns of action and internalize or automate them through repetition.

5

Proven equilibric actions allow us to perform the act of assimilation.

5.01

The totality of internalized successful strategies (satisfying our needs) constitute our (now long-tested) readiness-to-act structure, through which we are equipped with a certain number of possibilities for action.

5.02

For example, we handle or solve new mathematical problems with our already tested and internalized mathematical intelligence.

5.03

Or we behave emotionally toward others in ways that have satisfied both us and them in the past.

5.1

In general, then, we perceive reality through the glasses of an inner model of reality already tested by previous success, and interpret and interact with reality *through* this inner model and through the range of possible actions associated *with* this inner model.

5.2

So we encounter and counter each time-new reality in a way that is consistent with our already constructed model of reality. In this sense, we conform each time-new reality to the structures of our already existing reality.

5.3

We call each such act *assimilation*.

6

Perturbations that cannot be assimilated must/ should be eliminated sooner or later by our accommodation to the perturbing cause; by the act of accommodation.

6.1

What happens when an assimilating act is unable to restore our equilibrium state after a perturbation?

6.11

If we see someone crying, we may have learned through our development that we should comfort that person and ask them to stop crying, since we have behaved that way before with success; the person was satisfied afterwards....

6.12

But what if we do the same thing in a similar situation and the person reacts angrily to us because she does not want to stop crying?

6.21

Or we can figure out how much is two-thirds of two-quarters of a pie;

6.22

but what do we do when we are a little over-whelmed with picturing and looking through how much is seven ninths of two fifths of four sevenths?

6.23

What does a small child do when it first realizes with amazement that a cookie is not bendable like bread?

6.24

What happens cognitively in a believer who be-lieves in the omnipotence of a supernatural being but *cannot now resolve the claim* that no one can create a stone heavier than he can lift?

6.3

The reason for crying, the multiplication of fractures, the unbendability of the cookie, the impossibility of an omnipotence, or a psychologically difficult to bear altered reality and much more; in all these not easily surmountable cases of perturbation there are three possibilities of reaction.

6.31

The first, *assimilation*, does not bring much, the perturbation remains, because the new information blows up our previous "software" of possibilities of action.

6.32

The second is to *leave* the perturbation *unchanged*; but the already caused disturbance of our inner order will then remain and so an imbalance - with all its possible consequences - sticks in us..

6.33

In the third possibility, we *transform ourselves*. This time *we are* the ones who *adapt* to the reality of the new perturbation that cannot be assimilated.

6.41

Adapting in this direction is what we call *accommodation*.

6.42

The act of accommodation consists in either *rearranging* the psychocognitive (and thus physical) structure that we are, or expanding it with *new con-*

tent and *new relations*, or both, so that the range of our possibilities for action is qualitatively *transformed* or *grows* by new psychocognitive dimensions.

7

Essential learning consists in accommodation. Experience in accommodation enriches our life intelligence.

7.01

Certainly we can learn, i.e. change our knowledge, by accumulating more information; e.g. we can acquire the names of more capitals of this world;

7.02

such an act of learning, however, does not require any particular change in our psychocognitive structure, for we can learn new capital city names in the same way as those we already know, in a way that is already familiar, that is, by assimilative acts. Not so in the examples above (6.2).

7.1

Essential learning requires *accommodations*.

7.2

Accommodations require *restructuring* and thus a *fundamental transformation* and *qualitative growth* of the psycho-cognitive structure *that we are*, i.e.

our *identity*.

7.3

Thus, accommodative learning is more formative and existential because it changes our living *beingness*.

7.4

Last but not least, *essential learning* consists in *accommodating* because it is only through accommodating that we can come to know and *live* the *true extent* of our still dormant potential.

7.5

Assimilating and accommodating are acts that organismically equilibrate us after perturbations (equilibrium disturbances).

7.6

Very often we grow by *balancing* new "perturbations" of reality with accommodations, by *adapting* to the "disturbance" of this reality.

7.7

Once such accommodations have taken root, they

expand our assimilative range of action. But more importantly:

7.8

The richer our accommodating intelligence, the more prepared we are for the unexpected of the multi-shapeability of reality.

18.

About Mastering

1

As human beings, we are provided and *equipped* with physical, psychological and cognitive abilities for the nature and reality in which we came into being and exist.

1.1

By our nature we can *feel* and *perceive* with multiple senses.

1.11

Our feeling includes multiple *dimensions of sensing* and the more holistic faculty of *consciousness*.

1.2

We are by nature living energy and therefore have *desires*, *emotions* and *moods*, *likes* and *dislikes*, *appetites for many things*, *multiple needs*, and both a *multidimensional will* and a *self-willed will to live*.

1.3

We have *imagination*, we can *reflect* on what we perceive and experience, we have the ability of *logical thinking*.

1.4

Last but not least, we can *store* and *retrieve* received information through *memory*.

2

We can *realize our possibilities of life* through the *interaction of all our faculties with the substance and the working of reality, as* this reality results from our planetary and historical-cultural origin.

2.1

We live and exist in a cosmic-planetary world dimension.

2.2

Our particular and unique human character arises, on the one hand, from our planetary-ecological-biological *nature* and, on the other hand, from the *experiences* within our *life epoch*, that is, the historical and cultural time sphere into which we have been born.

2.3

Our reality consists of the <u>material</u>, of matter or energy, and of the <u>active</u>, of the forces and laws, which maintain, influence or determine everything material.

2.31

All this material and active is within *that*, which we call the space of the world or the *cosmic space*.

2.4

We also consist as human being of material and *we also* have forces with which we can operate and influence in many ways.

2.5

Our human life and being is caused and determined in its happening and course to a large extent by a totality of reality which is not subject to our control.

2.51

Therefore, we do *not* have *absolute* control of our lives.

2.6

However, we do have a relative control of our life.

2.61

Consciously or unconsciously, we can act in many ways and thereby cause and determine processes and parts of reality that influence or even often clearly shape the events and course of our life as a whole and in individual facets of it.

3

Life mastery is the sufficient, complete, or very high ability to *fulfill* the *necessities of life* and to *realize* as many of life's inherent *valuable possibilities* as is feasible and appropriate.

3.11

To *cause* and *determine* the happening, course, or mode of existence of something is to *control* that something.

3.12

And to be able to *control* the happening, course or mode of existence of something is to *master* that something.

3.21

To be able to control or master, for example, is to be able to control bicycling or our interactions with other people and other living beings or the organized course of our daily lives or to be able to freely express our emotions or or...

3.211

The list of all the facets we can master or control in

our lives is long.

3.22

But as soon as it is not about controlling or mastering one or more single facets in our life, but about our life as a whole, we talk about *mastering life*.

3.3

Mastering life has *two* dimensions.

3.31

We master life when we *fulfill* the *necessities* that life demands of us. Such necessities are usually rather indispensably existential than superfluously luxurious.

3.32

And we also master life when, *in addition*, we *unfold* and *achieve* many *valuable life possibilities* and *life realities*.

3.4

If we *master both* to a *sufficient*, *complete* or *very high degree*, we thereby achieve *life mastery*.

3.5

Life mastery is the sufficient, complete, or very high ability to *fulfill* the *necessities of life* and to *realize* as many of life's inherent *valuable possibilities* as is feasible and appropriate.

4

The *degree* and *quality* of *life mastery* is determined by how *deeply* we have *internalized* the *most basic life skills*.

4.1

To have an ability or to be able for something means

4.11

to embody the physical, mental and spiritual *knowledge*,

4.12

and to have the *power*

4.13

to *do* or *be* something.

4.2

We can expand and strengthen *innate* abilities as well as acquire *completely new ones*.

4.3

If our ability or skill to do something is sufficient or complete or very high, we *master* that something.

4.4

The steps to achieving a high level in a skill and to mastering this skill are *understanding, practicing, experiencing, internalizing,* and *mastering.*

4.5

The most basic skills that make up life mastery are what I call *life skills.*

4.6

All mastery of life begins and is maintained by obtaining the *energy resources* we need to live and act. This can also be considered the most important life necessity that we must be able to fulfill.

4.7

To *be able to fulfill* everything that is *necessary* for a life that is relaxed to an average degree, and to be *independent in it,* basically constitutes *adulthood.*

4.8

Action intelligence and *self-reliance* are the two life skills that make up the *qualifying core of adulthood.* Apart from these two, there are *another eighteen* most basic life skills.

4.9

The total of twenty most basic life skills are:

4.91

Relaxational intelligence, feeling intelligence, and authenticity.

4.92

Attentional intelligence, motivational intelligence, and emotional intelligence.

4.93

General intelligence and behavioral intelligence.

4.94

Communicational intelligence and language intelligence.

4.95

Groundedness and realism.

4.96

Rationality and pragmatism.

"Not everything is shining,
but everything that shines is."

Dreyfus/Kelly

4.97

Action intelligence and self-reliance.

4.98

Learning intelligence and organizational intelligence.

4.99

Contentment and freedom.

5

Beyond adulthood, life mastery also means *life fulfillment through contentment*, which consists in *nourishment, tranquility, wholeness* and *freedom*.

5.0

Our lives can take place under more favorable circumstances or under more difficult ones.

5.1

Even in the case of life under rather more difficult circumstances, which are (above all) beyond our control, *substantial life knowledge* is crucial and decisive, even *necessary* and *exceedingly valuable*.

5.2

If, however, we are fortunate enough to live under elementarily *more favorable* circumstances, substantial life knowledge contributes to the *realization of a fulfilling life*.

5.3

A fulfilling life is characterized by the fact that our lives are permeated with *contentment*.

5.4

We achieve contentment through the state and feeling of *nourishment, tranquility, wholeness* and *freedom*.

6

True life mastery involves the *vibrantly living* and *therefore* masterful *knowledge* of (1) *how reality "ticks"* or *works* and (2) *how to achieve organismic freedom.*

6.01

What *mastery* means, namely *the deeply internalized ability for something through sufficient understanding, practice and experience*, is clear.

6.02

What *is important to master*, which *life skills* namely, this is also clear, as these skills arise through life itself and are required or "demanded" by life.

6.1

However, (a) *life mastery*, as well as (b) *life skills*, and (c) the act of *mastering itself* are *not ends in themselves*, but life realization *intelligence*:

6.11

Life realization includes, first of all, *sustaining* life. And for this, *basic needs* must be *met* and *remain met* on a *cyclical and continual* basis.

6.12

To life-realization belongs as second the *unfolding* of life. And for this, the *higher order needs* must be *fulfilled* and *remain* fulfilled *cyclically and continuously.*

6.2

The *fulfillment* of all human needs enables and ensures the respective state of *nourishment* on every level, *physically, mentally-emotionally and spiritually* that is.

6.3

Life fulfillment and therefore life contentment is equivalent to the state of *holistic and complete nourishment.*

6.4

When we are holistically and completely nourished, we are organismically *free* because we are *content, at peace*, at rest within ourselves, and *vibrating without reaction*.

6.5

It is therefore important that we know our needs, remain aware of them, and organize our lives toward their fulfillment.

6.6

In order to organize our life holistically, we can/must act in many ways and thereby cause, determine and govern processes and parts of reality that influence or even often clearly shape the events and the course and development of our life as a whole and in individual facets of it (2.6).

6.7

If we are to be able to successfully cause, determine and govern processes and parts of reality, we must internalize, through *vibrantly-living* and *feeling experience, perception and reflection*, the knowledge *of how human* reality as well as *the whole* of reality *"ticks"*, according to which *unchanging laws and truths* it thus *"works"* or *acts* and *takes place*, because *this* reality can be *relied* upon.

Organismic *freedom*, the state that results from *holistic and complete nourishment* and in which we are *content, at peace, at rest within ourselves, and vibrating without reaction*, may also lead to "spiritual" or *transcendental-existential realization* or *actualization*.

7.1

Freedom as a *state* is *organismic* freedom, a contentedly and vibrantly restful and nourishing state of *wholeness*.

7.11

The organismic state of freedom occurs when *all basic physical, psychological, and mental needs are satisfied* and thus life is *fundamentally* mastered, and when the needs *unique to a particular person are satisfied* and thus that person's *humanness fully unfolds and occurs*.

7.12

Such an outcome of organismic freedom is true *success* in life, because it fulfills the *meaning* of life, which is that the life which we are takes place *as it is meant to by its nature.*

7.2

Wholeness <u>in the sense of *completeness*</u> – *com-pleteness-wholeness* – *means living in the com-pleteness and undividedness of one's nature and purpose of existence.*

7.3

And wholeness <u>in the sense of *well-being*</u> *– well-be-ing-wholeness – means the shining of one's own na-ture and purpose of existence.*

7.31

If organismic freedom (7.1) makes *complete-ness-wholeness* possible, then holistic realization of clarity, liberation and nourishment through the *being-realization of the essence of reality* makes possible a *transcendentally* holistic *well-be-ing-wholeness*, which is also called *enlightenment* or *transcendental existential realization*.

7.32

Such *transcendental*-holistic well-being-wholeness means an *unsurpassable and unparalleled* nourish-ment and *tracelessly deep self-luminous* contentment, which "opens up" when *cosmic-organismic understanding, knowledge, embodiment and being takes place sufficiently and happens fully.*

7.33

For this, too, the twenty most important life skills are means and compass, this time with a *boundlessly expanded* or *transcendentally holistic* radius of influence and impact.

7.4

Completeness-wholeness and well-being-wholeness are the state of *true fullness of life and existence* and therefore the strongest *attractors and motivators* of all acting, feeling, thinking and being.

7.5

Mastering, as a master act of living and being, even if it may have *manifold* and *isolated* spheres of activity, it cannot be in any way other than always being illuminated and guided by the suns of *completeness-wholeness* and *well-being-wholeness* in the accomplishment of life mastery.

7.6

The suns of *completeness-wholeness* and *well-be-ing-wholeness* illuminate the sky and the cosmic space of an (1) unconditional, (2) one's-self-contain-ing-nourishing-and-dissolving and (3) basic-exis-tentially-blissful and "unbearably" ecstatic *infinity-of-feeling-and-being-a-yes*, which is called *love*.

7.7

Consciously using our two *most important* resourc-es for this, namely *time* and *attention*, is really worth it.

7.8

Completeness-wholeness and well-being-whole-ness mean the existence *of* and *in* love.

7.9

Completeness-wholeness and well-being-whole-ness enable the existence *of a luminously vibrant aliveness in and as love.*

Part IV:

Vibrancy And

Radiance

19. Suffering And Reality

Yes, over and over again there are people who are satisfied with their lives. In the same way, many in this world - again and again - not only do not feel satisfied, well, at times many even feel quite tormented; or burdened with senseless suffering.

Wanting so much. Not getting enough. Struggling. Fighting.

Losing what is loved. Experiencing destruction of created.

Being careful what is allowed to say. Despairing of not having anyone, or rarely having anyone, to whom one can say everything without boundaries. Let alone to be able to feel without boundaries. With others. In front of others.

To be alone or to be together? To be or not to be? And *how* to be?

With such thoughts or statements we could join, among others, the Buddhist truth that suffering is the rule - or in some way predominant - in human life; and that whoever doubts this truth is not realistic enough; or either has not yet assembled the necessary neuronal synapses of an actual adult, or did not look that closely when assembling.

"Oh!", an opposite opinion faction could promptly retort: "Don't be wimps. Do you want to continue living with illusions? Fine. Here you go. Just don't complain when reality keeps interfering. Or else you go for a few lively walks, you take a good look at the world, you don't flee from what you can see and feel, and after you realize what makes the world tick, then you live fully. Nothing more, nothing less."

What makes the world tick? What world? Or: what exactly is meant by it? What is the world? Doesn't it depend on the perspective? Or does it just go far beyond that? What is reality? How to deal with the suffering in it? And how is full or fulfilling life possible?

20. The Bad And The Good

There is certainly always both bad news and good news. Or circumstances. Or situations. Both personal and individual, and societal and global. It always depends on which perspective you take. And there are many of them. I'll pick out two.

One of the many sad facts in the world, both historically and presently, is humanity's lack of development. Or viewed in another way: the discontent of humans. Or the problematic condition of humans. Not of each individual human being. But on the large scale.

That concerns for example the global destruction of the living foundations for exactly living organisms, once for the humans themselves and then also for all other living and feeling beings. Destruction of the environment. Production of unnecessary stuff. Blind growth compulsion. The blind, dark world will of Schopenhauer comes to my mind here.

And now let's take one of the more positive perspectives. Certain statistical facts indicate that we have made progress historically after all. Compared to other centuries, poverty has been greatly reduced, most people - in certain countries - belong to the middle class, and almost everyone - nine out of ten - under 25 is literate.

No doubt about it. Many things have improved compared to the longer past.

So are we humans already progressing? Or are we not? Has everything gotten better or worse? Or both? So has much become better and much worse at the same time?

Or is this still different view perhaps the more correct one? That we have developed technologically very much? Along with pleasant life consequences? And that there are morally and interhumanly and politically partly great improvements? And that at the same time we don't necessarily feel happier than people used to? Or that we have not necessarily developed further in terms of a fulfilling existence emotionally and perhaps also mentally, spiritually or existentially?

And finally, who has proven at all that evolution in the sense of the natural selection theory (if this is true overall) always means a good, even better further development? Provided that there is agree-

ment about what is the better or the good. So what
is the good?

21. The Nature Of The Good Life

What is or would be good, we already have an idea of that; always. Don't we? Our biology already directs us unmistakably towards everything we need. And what we need can only be good.

Is there any doubt or need to know that water is good, especially when we are thirsty? And isn't that enough of an example to support the *biologically generally* good?

Good is what we need biologically, but when in its natural or gently processed form it supports, promotes, sustains, fulfills our organismic completeness-wholeness and well-being-wholeness; and enables and nourishes it in general.

If we then reflect on different ways on satisfying our needs, then we are already reflecting on what is the good life or a good life as a whole. Emotionally. Spiritually. Physically. Holistically.

It is part of our nature that we are only truly there and fully vibrating in our *aliveness*, that is, in the state in which we are whole-bodily permeated by an energizing to uplifting nourishment that comes about through the nurturing of all dimensions of our human organismicity.

Such holistic nourishment thus enables primal-natural wholeness or the energetic shining and vibrating in the *fullness* designed by our *nature*, because all human-organismic needs are *satisfied* by the respective energy quality which is appropriate to them.

This kind of satisfaction of needs allows us to enter into the *peace* of the existential state of *contentment*, which can also be equated with the state of *organismic freedom*.

The state of organismic freedom is *self-luminous*, because only in it we are the deepest, because most free, *allowedness* and *existence-wanting-itself* and therefore also complete *affirmation* of life and existence.

Affirmation – or saying, feeling and being a Yes – means nothing else than the feeling or showing of the wanting to be and exist together with something. And fundamentally-existential-blissful affirmation to something is *love* for something. And affirmation as a state is the in-love *state*.

So it is part of our nature that only *in and as*

aliveness are we truly there and fully *vibrating*, and it is *equally* part of our nature that only <u>in</u> *and* <u>as</u> *love* do we truly exist and *shine* freely.

Vibrancy And Radiance

↑

Aliveness And Love

↑

Wholeness And Well-Being

↑

Contentment And Freedom

↑

Life Nourishment

↑

Life Mastery

↑

Master Acts Of Life And Life Skills

↑

Feeling And Needing

↑

Life And Reality

Life Mastery Decoded

"Yoga is union. The eternal spirit dwells in the cave of the body. When the two merge – that is yoga."

Nityananda

22. The Embodiment Of The Life Forces

We are an *energetic manifestation*. The energetic manifestation that we are *comes* to its destiny, that is, to take place completely, if the *forces* necessary and intended for it are *not* disturbed or confused, let alone *stopped*, in their unfolding, in their flow, in their working and in their vibrational field.

We have to *take care* of that. Certainly within the actual radius of our possibilities. And in no case by denial or violation of human, other-organismic and worldly laws and regularities.

We must dissolve that which worries us, and obtain that which deepens and completes our contentment and freedom, our wholeness and well-being.

Although *all* of the twenty most important life skills are indispensable for this purpose, they all center primarily around two core skills out of the twenty: namely, the skills of *feeling* and *action intelligence*.

Because the more fundamental of the twenty

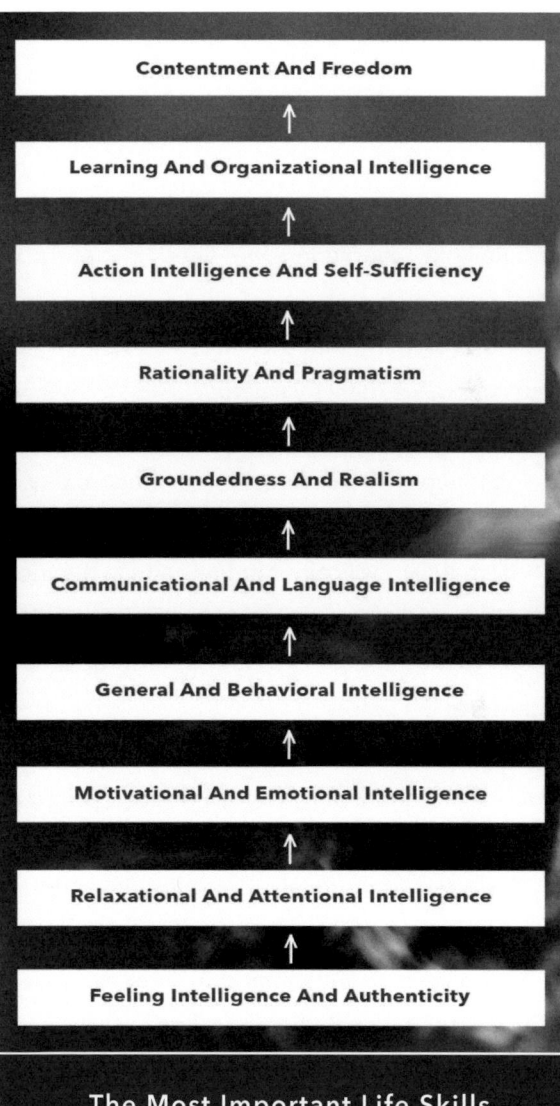

Contentment And Freedom

↑

Learning And Organizational Intelligence

↑

Action Intelligence And Self-Sufficiency

↑

Rationality And Pragmatism

↑

Groundedness And Realism

↑

Communicational And Language Intelligence

↑

General And Behavioral Intelligence

↑

Motivational And Emotional Intelligence

↑

Relaxational And Attentional Intelligence

↑

Feeling Intelligence And Authenticity

The Most Important Life Skills

life skills are only made possible, illuminated and dynamized *by* the feeling intelligence skill, and all the others basically compose the entire makeup of *action intelligence*.

If our *feeling* intelligence is intact, open, pure, and infallible, everything we need is clearly revealed.

And everything that we need, the totality of our needs that is, we fulfill by *acting*:

- as we should, and

- as much as the circumstances of our reality allow it,

- both daily, cyclically, routinely and in the more short-term mode...

- as well as in pursuit of longer-term goals and longer-term life paths.

We are energy. If we focus this energy physically, mentally or spiritually, we can direct it purposefully to create a movement or vibration.

This directed or directed energy with which we create movement and vibration is called *force*.

To feel this, to understand it, to experience it and to master it, enables us to *embody* the forces of life in a balanced, tuned and coherent way.

23. Primal Life Force Emotion

The coherent, tuned and balanced embodiment of life forces is a summary of everything that must be done when it comes to mastering life.

And life mastery we achieve first when we fulfill the necessities of life and thus the core of adulthood through intelligence of action and self-reliance, and we then deepen our life mastery in its degree and quality when we realize some, many or all of the life dimensions that make life more valuable and fulfilling through deeper mastery and dynamization of the most important life skills, through a more mature adulthood and growth, in other words.

In all this happening, one human reality dimension stands out *in particular*: the existence and the meaning of *emotions* and *emotionality*. Because: Emotions are not *everything*, but without emotions everything is *nothing*. Without them, the pleasant and the unpleasant would not exist. And the pleasant and the unpleasant determine the essence and quality of our being, generate all motivations and therefore guide all our actions.

Where do our emotions come from? Or what is their source?

Aliveness and love make up our existential *nature* and always fully occur and vibrate because of our *completeness-wholeness* and *well-being-wholeness*.

As our primal modes of existence, aliveness and love constitute our *most natural* and blissfully desiring-*itself*-state.

When both are intact and complete in their being, unclouded *comfort* or *happiness* occurs.

If both are endangered or disturbed, *fear* and possibly *pain* arise, whereby fear is almost always fear <u>of</u> physical or psychological <u>pain</u>.

A milder form of fear is *worry*. A milder form of pain is *discomfort*.

The spectrum of pain includes varying degrees of grief and psychological discomfort or unease as well as a range of physical-energetic pain.

Aliveness and love, as primal modes of existence and basic states of being, are the primal substance from which all other energetic states, emotions and inner feeling states arise, depending on what level of love and aliveness are present and tangibly existent or not.

For example, anger arises when the level of love is at significantly *less* than a medium level and at the same time the level of aliveness is at significantly *more* than a medium level.

An opposite example would be equanimity, which results from a higher level of love and a lower level of aliveness.

Thus, all emotions are derived from love and aliveness, and through this origin they become illuminated and transparent.

Understanding emotions and recognizing their importance and significance for a successful and fulfilling life, paying attention to them and taking them into account through acting and being, constitutes the essence of emotional intelligence. Emotional intelligence is the experiential knowledge about the importance of (especially) one's own emotions and about an appropriate way of dealing or/and being with them.

And if emotional intelligence is enriched with the ability of *empathy*, namely the ability to more or less feel the state of *another* living being, this strengthens our *behavioral* intelligence.

Each emotional state shapes and determines

our subjective and personal experience of reality, sometimes slightly, sometimes clearly, and sometimes radically.

Difficult emotions hinder us, paralyze us, sadden us.

Pleasant emotions make us happy, nourish us, inspire us.

A true mastery of life requires emotional knowledge and skill, just as oxygen belongs to our lungs and water to our body. Such knowledge and skill is the psychic oxygen of a successful and valuable life.

24. Adulthood And Transcendence

Emotional skill and knowledge are not always sufficient, especially when the limits of what is bearable and feasible for our organismic existence are exceeded.

And even if such knowledge could be sufficient under normally tolerable conditions, unfortunately it is not sufficiently promoted in the education and upbringing system.

Emotional intelligence, however, would have to be taught and internalized as the most important quality. In the same way, feeling intelligence would have to be taught and internalized. And also behavioral intelligence. And ideally all the most important life skills and master acts of life. From the very beginning.

Because already during childhood, or especially during infancy, the soil must be fertile for a personality to take root. Likewise during puberty and adolescence.

With strong roots, growth and development

are then advanced into the dimensions of becoming and being an adult.

Beyond foundational adulthood, which consists of being able to take care of our lives self-reliantly and mastering appropriate behavior for our togetherness with others, there are additional, higher and deeper levels of adulthood or levels of growth:

For a more nurturing togetherness. For different facets of a more satisfying creativity. For a more meaningful penetration and understanding of reality. For a more assured achievement of personal self-realization. Intellectually. Spiritually. Physically.

And not least - if this is felt as an unmistakable need - for a spiritually or existentially-transcendentally truthful life.

All this is not guaranteed at all. But it is possible; and it is all the more certain, the more convincingly and certainly we answer the following seven questions with a clear and holistically-organismically felt *yes*.

Do we know - according to the human capacity - the real conditions and the laws of the entire and the human reality?

Is our feeling capacity – as a compass for everything we need – clear and unclouded?

Is our level of internalization of the most important life skills and the master acts of life deep enough?

Are we fulfilling all our needs in such a way that a foundational life nourishment is attained?

Or are we even reaching such a deep life nourishment that constitutes a restful life contentment and an organismic freedom?

So, through all of this, do we come to our completeness-wholeness and well-being-wholeness in large part or completely as it is intended to be by our nature?

Are we thereby released into a free vibrancy and radiance as aliveness and love?

Epilogue

The Twofold Meaning Of Life

Free and regardless of any form of meaning given by an organized religion, by a cultural normativity, by a political ideology or by any differently derived worldview, there is one or *the* meaning of life, which is undoubtable and self-evident.

We are an organismic-energetic manifestation of nature and reality. We come to the world with growth potentials and unfoldment possibilities laid out in us.

The organismic-energetic nature and reality manifestation that we are occurs fully when we unfold our possibilities and actualize our potentials, and when the life that we are is expressed, takes place, and vibrates as it is inherently meant to; whether that is expressed in, for example, drinking water when we are thirsty, or creating something when we feel the urge to do so, or striving for nurturing relationships when we feel the deep need to exist in love, or wanting to move and exercise physically, or simply abiding and existing in a satisfying experience, or, or, or. ..

The first and *undoubtable* meaning of life is *life*

itself and its *being lived* in all its facets, realms and dimensions.

If the life that we are is *not* lived as it is meant to be by nature and by lawful reality, then an inner *restlessness* prevails within us that can take on the most diverse forms of dissatisfaction, disturbance and disease.

Of course, for every person there is always an additional meaning in life, or even more than one additional meaning, if a certain purpose or talent or accomplishment in a certain area is connected with it. However, even in this case, such an additional meaning of life is a part of the will-to-be-lived of the life of the respective particular person.

Now, when I speak of a truly different *second* meaning of life, namely, the realization of the *divinely pervaded life*, which is *therefore* the *most attractive* because it is *nourishment* itself, *fullness* itself, and *love* itself, this is an *open* statement, because such a life is *not* accessible *to all*, or because for many it may signify a merely dreamy and illusory *fantasy*.

By 'divine' here is meant nothing less than the innermost, most free, most nourishing, omnipresent and all encompassing, pervading and being *essence* of unconditional *reality*, *free* from religions and spiritual doctrines, and given *by itself*.

In the meaning of 'divine' meant here, then, a divinely pervaded and nourished life represents the *possible* second meaning of life; the possible and *not certain* meaning of life, because it is not easy to fulfill even for all those who feel a truly genuine, unspoiled and illusion-free need for it. Very often this results on the one hand from a *missing knowledge*, and on the other hand again from a strong and counterproductive *cultural conditioning*.

The life mastery outlined, presented, and decoded in this book contains the foundational, essential and decisive knowledge to approach and *fulfill* both the one *and the other* meaning of life.

Glossary

ability: embodying the physical or/and mental or/and emotional knowledge, and also having the power and being in the circumstance of doing or being something.

achieve: to bring something to existence by being or doing.

actualizing tendency: the innate urge to unfold, realize and be what is inherently in us, as it is touched, nourished and dynamized by the natural laws of reality.

adult: a fully grown person, self-sufficient in life and responsible for his or her own actions.

affection: the feeling state of wanting to come closer to something or wanting to be with something.

attention: directed consciousness.

attention intelligence: the experiential knowledge of the causes of movement and of the nourishing sources of one's attention.

authentic: belonging to the sensed real.

authenticity: the way of being that results from the respective sensed reality of all that expresses itself naturally and unhindered as our entire organismicity: as the "universe" of the energy flow of the perpetual cycle of being-sensing-needing-getting-becoming-being...

autonomous: free and independent to be, decide and act according to one's own principles and laws.

autonomy: the freedom and independence to be, decide and act according to one's own principles and laws.

calculate: to find out how much something is when it is compared with something of its kind.

capable: having the ability.

change (1): the process by which something becomes different.

change (2): the process by which something becomes different or new in time in its form or/and composition or/and quantity or/and arrangement.

change (3): quantitative or/and qualitative transformation or transformation of energetic arrangements or manifested configurations.

civilization (1): the totality of valuable accumulated knowledge with the purpose of good human coexistence.

civilization (2): through education emerged human way of being and living.

communication: the happening in which information is sent and/or received between sentient and cognitive beings.

communicative intelligence: the experiential knowledge and the ability, based on it, to communicate appropriately and effectively and to deal with what is communicated.

contentment: the state and feeling of nourishment, tranquility, wholeness and freedom.

control (1): the power over something.

control (2): the causing or/and directing of a way of being or happening of something.

control (3): overseeing the way something exists or happens.

control (1): to have power over something.

control (2): to cause or/and direct the way of being or happening of something.

control (3): to oversee how something exists or happens.

create (1): to bring something to material existence.

create (2): to bring something into existence by being or doing.

cybernetics: the science of steering or directing (Greek: kyberno = to steer, navigate; Sanskrit: kubara = steering wheel of a means of motion).

decide (1): to commit to one of two or more possibilities of fulfillment of a need or necessity.

decide (2): to determine.

direct: to cause the direction of movement of

something.

emotion (1): a more or less pleasant or unpleasant powerful feeling.

emotion (2): inner energetic space, which results from a known or unknown reason/cause, and which, depending on the proportions and the kind of excitability, inertia and calmness, results in a certain mood/condition of the way of being or/and the readiness for activity and behavior of a living being capable of evaluating.

emotion (3): the more or less pleasant or unpleasant quality or inner existential atmosphere of the feeling state of a living being.

emotional intelligence: the experiential knowledge of the meaning of one's own emotions and of how to deal or/and be with them appropriately.

empathy: the ability to feel the state of another living being.

enlightenment (1): an intellectual movement and attitude (originated between the 17th and 18th century) that is based on rationality and autonomous thought, judgement and decision making.

enlightenment (2): holistic clarity.

enlightenment (3): holistic clarity, liberation and nourishment through the realization of the essence of reality.

equilibrium: the state of balance (Latin: aequi = equal + libra = weight).

ethics: the totality of all laws and rules that govern human action and behavior in interaction with others.

experience: conscious sensing and experiencing through organismic being touched by the existence, vibration and movement of reality.

family (1): a group of living beings that form a nourishing whole for biological or other important reasons.

family (2): group.

feel: to notice an energetic arrangement or transformation psychically or/ and physically.

feeling (1): the sensed or felt inner state of a person or other living being.

feeling (2): faculty of sentient perception and cognition.

feeling faculty: the capability of feeling.

free: the quality of feeling state in which we feel no internal or external constraints and/or limitations or restrictions and/or necessities.

freedom: the feeling state in which we feel no internal or external constraints and/or limitations or restrictions and/or necessities.

freedom, organismic: the state in which we exist as a free self and feel the unhindered realization of our actualizing tendency.

friendship: a relationship between two people containing trust, affection and love for each other.

fulfill: to cause completely the condition for an existence or for something to happen.

fulfilled: to be full of something.

fulfillment (1): the existing of something after the conditions for it have been caused.

fulfillment (2): emotional nourishment.

fully: in a high or in the highest degree of something.

goal: the final state or place of a movement or action.

grounded: rooted in the intelligence of the laws of reality and thus of the laws of life as well.

groundedness: rootedness in the intelligence of the laws of reality and thus of the laws of life as well.

happiness: the feeling state filled with a high or highest degree of satisfaction and euphoria.

holistic: relating to a whole or to the whole of something.

importance: the composition or/and quality of something, determined by the degree to which it fulfills a need or necessity.

important: something that has importance.

insight: spontaneously arising content of knowledge, cognition, understanding or thinking.

intelligence (1): naturally available or retrievable stored knowledge coupled with the ability to see through, understand, figure out, learn, know something new for oneself and in its possible relationships to others.

intelligence (2): knowledge or/and information.

joy: internally felt euphoric energy.

knowledge (1): naturally available and to-something-enabling living information or totality of information.

knowledge (2): the totality of everything a living being learned or/and experienced.

language intelligence: the mastery of appropriate words and forms of expression to describe content of perceiving, feeling, experiencing, thinking and knowing.

law(s) of humans: manner of conduct decided and established by nature or human beings and binding on all concerned.

law(s) of nature or reality: the unchanging way something exists and behaves.

learning: the process or experience that leads to new knowledge or/and being.

learning (autotelic learning): learning activity that is itself already the goal or/and fulfillment of its happening.

learning (organismic learning): change of knowledge or/and being determined by the total-organismic intelligence and generated by total-organismic experience.

learning cybernetics: the equilibrial control of the unmistaken direction of the learning process.

learning goal: the new state of knowing and/or being to be achieved through a learning process.

learning intelligence (1): the masterful knowledge of how learning works.

learning intelligence (2): the ability to (1) holistically recognize, perceive, feel, and understand (1.1) one's authentic motivation, (1.2) authentic reality, and (1.3) the relationship of one's authentic motivation to authentic reality, (2) fully design a living strategy to harmonize this relationship, and (3) steadfastly implement and fulfill the designed strategy.

life force: the power giving force to a living being.

life mastery: the sufficient, complete or very high ability to (a) fulfill the necessities of life and (b) realize as many of life's inherent possibilities as possible.

life skill: one of the skills necessary for a realized and contented life.

love (1): affection for something that is pleasant.

love (2): related or unrelated to someone or something (1) unconditional, (2) containing, nurturing, and dissolving one's self, (3) basic-existentially blissful and "unbearably" ecstatic infinity of feeling and being a yes.

luck: good or right conditions for something.

master: a person with a complete or very high ability in something.

master (1): being able to do or finish something difficult.

master (2): to keep something under control.

masterful: like a master.

mastery: the complete or very high ability in something.

meaning of life (1): the purpose of life itself.

meaning of life (2): the purpose of an individual life based on one's own design.

meaning of life (3): the purpose of an individual life on the basis of one's own actualizing tendency.

meaning of life (4): the purpose inherent in life of unfolding and realizing or actualizing the powers and dispositions that constitute life within and as an expression and happening of the most holistic pure reality possible.

motivatedness: the sensation of a need-generated restlessness.

motivation: a feeling state in which a moving force (originating from a motivatedness) towards something is sensed.

motivational intelligence: (a) the experiential knowledge of one's needs and (b) the sense of real life necessities coupled with (c) the ability to fulfill both.

need: the sensation of a state of deficiency and a concomitant restlessness and a simultaneous directedness toward the removal of that deficiency.

need: to feel a state of lack and a concomitant restlessness or a simultaneous directedness towards the removal of this lack.

order (1): the way something accidentally or purposefully is or becomes arranged.

order (2): the composition and set-up of one or more elements required by a particular system.

order (3): the appropriate condition.

organ: an in itself complete, integrated and a specific function fulfilling part of a living being.

organization (1): the act of organizing or/and an organizing event or the state of being organized.

organization (2): a group of living beings that relate to and act with each other in such a way as to accomplish a specific purpose or achieve a specific goal.

organize: to bring a system into such a favorable coherent arrangement that this system has a fluid functionality or all the characteristics of a healthy living organism, so that a certain purpose is fulfilled or a certain goal is achieved.

perceive: to consciously notice objects or elements of external or internal reality in their identity in a more or less concrete way by means of sentient faculties, such as the senses.

perception: the bipolar event by which a subject, i.e. a psychophysical recipient, becomes aware of the identity of objects or elements of external or internal reality in a more or less concrete way by means of sensory faculties, such as the senses.

practice: to do something longer and repeatedly in order to become better or very good at it.

pragmatism: the ability or/and way to orient and adapt to real situations and to the knowledge of how these can lead to success when there are problems to solve or goals to achieve.

precise: in every smallest detail in accordance with a requirement or expectation.

priority: precedence over something else.

prioritize: to list the stages of a multi-stage event or the individual items on a list in terms of their priority.

problem: small to high degree of interference or disturbance with the happening or existence of something.

purpose: the goal of an action or happening or process.

rational: possessing the property or ability of inferential reasoning.

rationality: the property or ability of inferential reasoning.

reach: to arrive at a place or time through movement or/and through a process.

read: to experience the content of a text through understanding.

realism: the ability or/and way to perceive things as they really are, without becoming or/and being influenced by beliefs, wishful thinking, uncertainty and hope.

reality: the totality of everything that exists.

realize (1): to recognize.

realize (2): to actualize something or cause something to come into real existence.

relaxation: the freeing of the inner energy flow from being held and pressed.

relaxational intelligence: the experiential knowledge of the different dimensions and the corresponding fulfillment processes of (a) one's nourishment and (b) the real necessities of life.

relaxedness: the freedom from the act and/or occurence of the holding and depressing of the inner energy flow and state.

responsibility: the natural or otherwise established right or authorization for something, i.e. the rightful and committing authorship for something.

responsible: to be in charge of something for which the authorship belongs to one or more persons either naturally or assigned by other arrangements.

result: that which is there or happens (directly and exclusively) next, after something that is there before or happens before.

rule: humanly decided and determined binding manner of behavior for all involved.

satisfaction: euphorically satiating state of a person or of a living being, which arises from the fulfillment of a need.

science: activity dedicated to the "generation" or/ and discovery of true knowledge.

scientific: anything dedicated to the "generation" or/and discovery of true knowledge.

self-sufficiency: being independent from others in the way to live and to exist and in causing all the necessary resources for the life.

self-sufficient: to be independent from others in the way to live and to exist and in causing all the necessary resources for the life.

sense (1): ability of sensation and perception associated with an organ of a living being.

sense (2): meaning or content of something.

sense: to feel something (more) subtly or most subtly in unobstructed consciousness.

sensing: ability of subtler and deeper feeling perception and recognition of something that is not directly or easily perceptible and recognizable.

skill: a higher or very high degree of an ability to

do something.

spell: to have the ability of writing words in the sequence of letters that make them up.

success: the good or/and valuable result of an activity or a process.

successful: the property of an activity or process that brings about success.

terminate: cause the end of an existence or happening.

time: the "length" of the existence of something or the "length" of a happening.

together: being within the presence or space of one or more persons or entities or things.

togetherness: to be so connected with or to be within the presence or space of one or more living beings, persons or entities or things, in a way, that instead of the feeling of being alone, there is or arises the sensed being part of a greater whole.

true (1): everything that is real.

true (2): everything that coincides with reality.

trust (1): the emotionally-mentally deep (and nurturing) state of knowledge and certainty toward a person or anything else at all, which is unmistakably reliable and benevolent in its true being and behavior toward the trusting person.

trust (2): sensed certainty of the correctness, truth or/and reliability of something.

truth (1): a property of the real.

truth (2): the coincidence of a statement or information with reality.

understanding: the perceiving or/and sensing or/and becoming of the identity, meaning, content or/and essence of something.

value: the degree of importance something has for a living being.

voluntary: pertaining to one's own and free will.

want: to feel motivational energy towards the fulfillment of a need.

wanting, true: real wanting that leads to action. We cannot feel it and remain passive and inactive at the same time. We recognize true wanting by restlessness. When I really want something, I recognize it by the fact that I become restless when I do not yet have or am not yet what I want. So restless that I automatically give in to the urge to move, which generates the necessary action that leads me to what I want.

whole (1): the quality of being such that everything necessary for one's existence is there and nothing is lacking.

whole (2): the quality in which something exists in the completeness and indivisibility of its nature and purpose of existence.

whole (1): something in which nothing necessary for its own existence is missing.

whole (2): something that exists in the completeness and indivisibility of its nature and purpose of existence.

wholeness: the quality or property of existing in the completeness and undividedness of one's own nature and existential purposefullness.

wholly: in a high or in the highest degree of something.

will: the directed total force that drives a living being to a mode of existence or/and being or/and effective action and arises from and through all respective needs.

wisdom: deeper to most profound knowledge acquired through experience and understanding.

Citation References

In the order the citations appear in this book

----

09   *Men first feel:* Vico (1948), 70

29   *We had no say:* Magee (2014), 111

77   *There is a difference:* Aristotle (330 BCE),

     Chapter 1

100 *Through organismic:* Rogers (1998), 124

127 *Every being has a:* Langer (2007), 19-20

151 *As the new people:* Willemsen (2006), 34

175 *My life is a story of:* Jung (1961), 10

201 *We are never finished in:* Roth (2019), 297

227 *Not everything is:* Dreyfus/Kelly (2015), 325

251 *Yoga is:* Nityananda (1996), 219

Literature

Aristotle, *Nicomachean Ethics*, Athens, 330 BCE.

Dreyfus/Kelly, *Alles, was leuchtet (All Things Shining)*, Berlin 2015.

Jung, Carl Gustav, *Erinnerungen, Träume, Gedanken (Memories, Dreams, Reflections)*, Zürich, Düsseldorf 1961.

Langer, Inghard, *Die Person als Mittelpunkt der Wirklichkeit (The Person As The Center Of Reality)*, Lernintelligenz-Magazin, Nr.3, Hamburg 2007.

Magee, Bryan, *Ultimate Questions*, Woodstock, Oxfordshire 2016.

Nityananda, (1897-1961), *The Sky Of The Heart*, Portland, Oregon 1996.

Rogers, Carl R., *Entwicklung der Persönlichkeit (On Becoming A Person)*, Stuttgart 1998.

Roth, Gerhard, *Warum es so schwierig ist, sich und andere zu ändern (Why It Is So Difficult To Change Yourself And Others)*, Stuttgart 2019.

Vico, Giambattista, *The New Science*, Ithaca, New York 1948.

Willemsen, Roger, *Wer wir waren (Who We Were)*, Frankfurt am Main 2006.

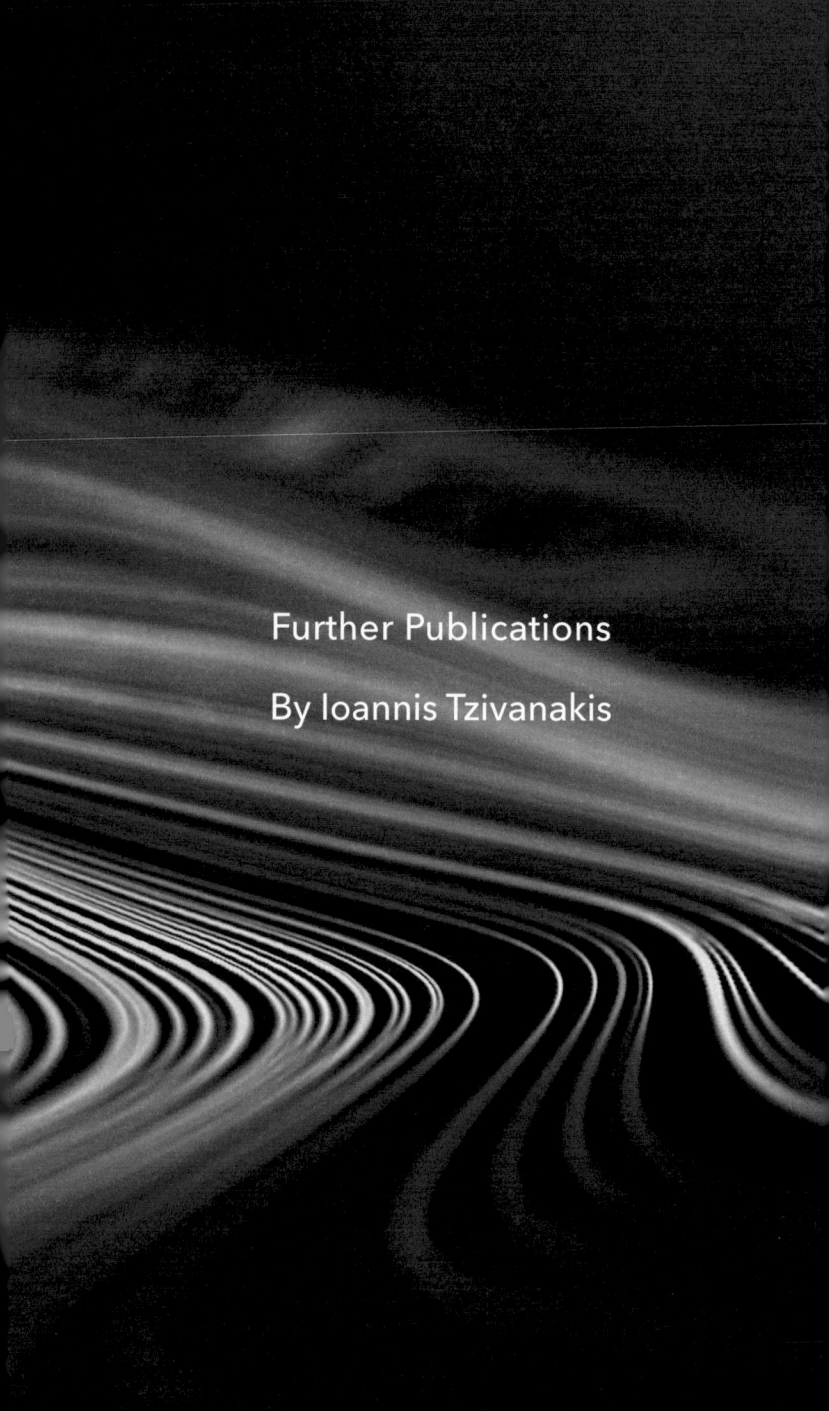

Further Publications

By Ioannis Tzivanakis

IOANNIS TZIVANAKIS

LEXICON OF LIFE

ITV

life skills mastery

IOANNIS TZIVANAKIS

Ioannis Tzivanakis

Attention Counseling

ITV

ADHD DECODED

IOANNIS TZIVANAKIS

THE SOURCES OF ADHD & THEIR
TRANSFORMATIVE POWER

Publisher: Ioannis Tzivanakis Verlag, Hamburg 2022.

Printed in Germany.

ISBN 978-3-940493-39-2

www.lifemasterydecoded.com

Bibliographic information published by the Deutsche
Nationalbibliothek (German National Library): The Deutsche
Nationalbibliothek lists this publication in the Deutsche
Nationalbibliografie (German National Bibliography).

About The Author

Ioannis Tzivanakis studied linguistics and philosophy of language at the University of Bremen. His main focus was semantics, consciousness research and holism.

Since 1996 he works as a trainer, coach and consultant in the areas of *Life Mastery*, *Life Skills*, *Spirituality*, *Learning Intelligence* and *ADHD* both in Germany and worldwide.

In 2006 and 2007 he published four issues of the Learning Intelligence Magazine on the topics of *learning foundations*, *learning intelligence*, *management* and *spirituality*.

His already published books are "ADHD Decoded" (2018), "Lexicon Of Life" (2021) and "Life Skills Mastery" (2022).

More information on his programs, courses, seminars and coaching areas can be found at:

www.tzivanakis.com